Zen Katha

Partap Sharma is a playwright, novelist (*Days of the Turban*) and author of four books for children. His best known plays, *A Touch of Brightness* and *Begum Sumroo*, have been staged in various countries. His books have been published in India, England, USA, France, Denmark, Holland and Canada. As an actor, he has played the lead in five Hindi feature films and won the National Award in 1971 for his performance in *Phir Bhi*. He has also played the role of Nehru in the film *Nehru: Jewel of India*. In the year 2003, he spent three months in China to take part, again as Nehru, in an international film titled *Chou-en-lai in Bandung*. He has directed a number of documentary films, including a historical series for Channel Four Television, London, titled *The Raj Through Indian Eyes*. As a result, England's Museum of the British Empire & Commonwealth, in Bristol, now has a permanent section devoted to film clips and interviews titled *The Partap Sharma Archive on the British Raj*. His voice is well-known to cinema, TV and radio audiences as he is one of India's foremost commentators and narrators. He is the recipient of the Dadasaheb Phalke Award.

By the same playwright

Begum Sumroo

Zen Katha

(inspired by the life of Bodhidharma, founder of zen and the martial arts)

A PLAY IN TWO ACTS

Partap Sharma

RUPA

Published by
Rupa Publications India Pvt. Ltd 2004
7/16, Ansari Road, Daryaganj
New Delhi 110002

Sales centres:
Allahabad Bengaluru Chennai
Hyderabad Jaipur Kathmandu
Kolkata Mumbai

Copyright © Partap Sharma 2004

All rights reserved.
No part of this publication may be reproduced, transmitted,
or stored in a retrieval system, in any form or by any means,
electronic, mechanical, photocopying, recording or otherwise,
without the prior permission of the publisher.

ISBN: 978-81-291-0564-6

Second impression 2014

10 9 8 7 6 5 4 3 2

The moral right of the author has been asserted.

Typeset by Nikita Overseas Pvt. Ltd., New Delhi

Printed at Saurabh Printers, Noida

This book is sold subject to the condition that it shall not, by way
of trade or otherwise, be lent, resold, hired out, or otherwise circulated,
without the publisher's prior consent, in any form of binding or cover
other than that in which it is published.

Contents

Acknowledgements ix

Characters 1

Act One 3

Act Two 62

*For my father who,
in life and death,
exemplified the spirit of zen.*

Acknowledgements

Research for this play has taken many years and generated many enthusiasms in me. My first acknowledgement is to the spirit of Bodhidharma, which happily sat lightly on the shoulder true to the way of zen, and led me into nine years of slog learning the martial arts. It was a change from the sedentary habits of writers doing academic research. Then, I must thank Sensei Pervez Mistry and all the others who taught me in his dojo. I no longer worry about my broken bones. Everything mends.

I consulted many scholars, read many books on the subject and, if I cannot name all two hundred of them here, I thank them nevertheless. In particular, I thank the historian Dr. (Mrs.) Kalpakam Sankarnarayan, an authority on the Buddhist period, who xeroxed an entire book and sent it to me. I am also indebted to Professor Jamkhedkar, scholar of Sanksrit and Pali, who discussed relevant details with me. And, of course, I am indebted to my dear friend Vinod C. Khanna (former Ambassador to Cuba, Bhutan etc.) for tactical and practical guidance on travelling in the footsteps of Bodhidharma.

In China, I was particularly encouraged by the keen interest of Shiv Shankar Menon who was then Indian Ambassador in Beijing and by Shyam Saran, the Indian Ambassador in Indonesia (subsequently Foreign Secretary), who gave me insights into the practice of zen meditation and the monastic way in the Far East, particularly in Japan.

Most of all, I must thank the Deputy Abbot who granted me a long, quietly humourous interview and, of course, the amazing monks of Shaolin-se.

Later, when I wished to communicate with Li Zhi, the Chinese artist renowned for his powerful depictions of Bodhidharma at Shaolin, it was my daughter Namrita who, through her friend Andrea Mingfai Chu in Shanghai, located the artist and obtained permission for us to use his magnificent painting on the cover of this book. To all of them my heartfelt thanks.

But I don't think I would have survived my research, my travels and my enthusiasms without the strong and warmly comforting understanding of my wife. I owe her...well, helluva lot. Meanwhile, I hope this play and my love will do.

Partap Sharma

Cast List

Zen Katha by Partap Sharma was first produced by the Primetime Theatre Company and directed by Lillete Dubey. It opened on 15 August 2004 at the Sophia Bhabha Hall, Mumbai, with the following cast:

Rajiv Gopalakrishnan	as	Bodhidharma
Sandhya Mridul, Anu Menon	as	Sangha
Denzil Smith	as	Prajna
Shardul Chaturvedi	as	Drishti & Fang Chang
Vikrant Chaturvedi	as	Vajra

Asif Ali Beg, Pallavi Symons and Pavan Singh played all the other characters.

The music was composed by Mahesh Tinaikar, the choreography was created by Mahesh Mahbubani. Martial arts consultant to the production was Shihan Pervez Mistry (7 Dan Black Belt).

Characters

PRAJNA	A Brahmin
DRISHTI	Chief of Army
DHARMA	Prince, later Bodhidharma
SANGHA	Daughter of Drishti
VAJRA	A rich, young merchant

The ensemble of actors will double up to play the incidental characters such as: Messenger, Tantric, Crowd, Guards, Referee, Green Headband, White Headband, Prince Nandivarman, Prince Shivavarman, Patriarch Prajnatara, Chinese Emperor, Courtiers, Old Chinese Woman, Hui K'o, Soldiers, Brigands, Abbot Fang Chang, Monks.

Act One

Scene 1

A silver cauldron of fire. Prajna the Brahmin is seated beside it, chanting Sanskrit mantras and, at intervals, ladling ghee onto the flames.

A messenger enters and holds up his hand for silence. Prajna stops chanting and rises anxiously. From somewhere within comes the feeble crying of a newborn child.

MESSENGER: Stop your *puja*! The King says the child is a weakling. He wants him put out of his misery.
PRAJNA: No, that cannot be.
MESSENGER: Why? The King desires it.
PRAJNA: It must not be. It's a sin to take life.
MESSENGER: What life are you talking about? [*Sarcastically*] The boy is premature, has difficulty breathing, goes blue in the face and seems likely to die in the next few hours.

PRAJNA: Krishna was blue too. Given a chance, the child can be taught to breathe.

MESSENGER: [*Laughs*] How can you teach a new-born anything?

PRAJNA: Abhimanyu learnt military strategy in his mother's womb. Learning begins before birth and continues in life.

MESSENGER: You argue too well for me, but I don't think you can convince the King. You know, the Pallavas of Kanchipuram pride themselves on their personal strength and wrestling skill.

PRAJNA: [*Smiles*] I learnt to wrestle too. It was part of growing up.

MESSENGER: But, for the Pallavas, it is part of the syllabus of kingship. Here, they are called 'mallas', wrestlers. They like that. That is why they have named their city Mamallapuram. The weight of such a past is enough to kill a child that cannot fight.

PRAJNA: I will teach him to be a fighter, the very best.

MESSENGER: [*Smirks*] If he survives.

PRAJNA: The King cannot predict the future. He is no astrologer.

MESSENGER: Are you?

PRAJNA: [*Hesitates, then takes the plunge*] From what you tell me, I see that the child only needs help to breathe. Then, moment to moment, day by day, he will gain in strength. [*Pauses and then as if making a decision*] Tell the King, I would like to bring him up as my own.

MESSENGER: You! But you are single. A poor, wandering Brahmin, here on the King's charity. How can you? [*Thinks. Then*] Unthinkable.
PRAJNA: [*Pacing about*] I am a man. I can be a father.
MESSENGER: Not to a king's son.
PRAJNA: If I cannot be a father to the child, let me be his teacher. That is the *dakshina*, the fee I ask of the King, for the ceremony I have performed.
MESSENGER: [*Nods*] I shall tell the King.
PRAJNA: And tell him, I would like to name the child Dharma. Because a Brahmin would rather part with his own life than his *dharma*.

The Messenger bows and withdraws.

Scene 2

A small clay lamp, burning on a silver salver. The little flame throws up giant shadows as the Tantric whirls on his feet, dishevelled, bearded, fearsome and gurgling with laughter.

Drishtivisha Chola, Chief of Army, enters.

DRISHTI: O Tantric, I need your help. The pandit is causing havoc with his mantras.
TANTRIC: [*Still whirling*] Ah, Drishtivisha Chola, you may be Chief of Army but know this: all of life is a battlefield … of philosophies.
DRISHTI: A battlefield of philosophies?

TANTRIC: [*Stops whirling*] Indeed. Look at your own behaviour. You've come to me because of some pandit's mantras. Because you believe as most people do, that pandits do white magic and tantrics do black. Well, let me tell you the truth. There is no white magic and there is no black. It's just that most of these pandits believe in a moral principle of the universe and tantrics don't. Tell me, do you believe in God, Drishti?

DRISHTI: Well, I ... er... am ... would like to be ... a good Buddhist and the noble eight-fold path enjoins us to right thinking, right action, right—

TANTRIC: Then why do you come to me when you want to ensure that a child is killed or a pandit put in his place? These are neither right thoughts nor right actions. [*Drishti is unsure whether he is being baited. The Tantric circles him*] You see, for these, and such, you come to a man who does not believe in good and evil. You come to a tantric — [*Moving around like a man possessed*] a mystical scientist, a herbalist who can with particular potions cure or kill. [*Swings round*] I explore knowledge beyond the boundaries of petty morality, because there is no moral principle in the universe. How you live does not affect the speed at which the planets are hurtling on to catastrophe.

DRISHTI: You are speaking at a tangent I cannot comprehend.

TANTRIC: [*Sighs*] Ah yes! This is too abstruse for you. Shall we move on to practical matters? Or would you like to have some group sex first?

DRISHTI: [*Shocked*] O Tantric!
TANTRIC: [*To Drishti*] For a military man you are easy to shock.
DRISHTI: Please be serious.
TANTRIC: Why? Nothing matters anyway. Why be serious?
DRISHTI: [*Quite fiercely*] It matters to us Cholas to recover our past glory from the clutches of the Pallavas. We must prevent them from consolidating their power. The death of this child is crucial to our purpose. You know that. We put our faith in you, but your plan didn't work.
TANTRIC: You mean, *you* failed to accomplish what was expected of you.
DRISHTI: [*Protests*] No. I did exactly as you advised. The moment the Queen died, I rushed to the King. I emphasized her death rather than the birth of the infant. I prodded at the King's grief. He was in deep anguish anyway. He had loved her dearly. When I talked of her many kindnesses, he trembled and turned his face away so I would not see 'a great Pallava' in tears.
TANTRIC: Yes, yes.... but the child. Come back to the child. How did you proceed?
DRISHTI: "This child is a mother-eater, Your Majesty, a womb-destroyer," I said. "It forced its way out before its time. It is evil." He didn't like that. He said 'It cannot be evil. It is *my* child.'
TANTRIC: [*Laughs*] Oh, typical, typical, typical Pallava!
DRISHTI: But then I said, "Hardly *your* child, Your Majesty. He is shrivelled and scrawny. A sort of tadpole. More

like a blue fish than a baby." That settled it. His Pallava pride boiled over and he roared, 'I'll have it destroyed.'

TANTRIC: So, as I foretold, he did give the order.

DRISHTI: Of course, and by now that Pallava pup would have been dead if that clever pandit had not convinced the King to let him live.

TANTRIC: So now this weakling may become Patriarch of Buddhism and there will be no boundaries to his kingdom. [*Gives a gurgling laugh*] Ah! The Queen was clever. Her first son was heir-apparent, the second was a standby so she converted to Buddhism and pledged a future son, if she had one, to the Patriarch! Today Pallava ships sail all the way to China for trade. Who knows but this third Prince might even help make all of China Buddhist!

DRISHTI: I would welcome that. But it should happen under us Cholas, not under the Pallavas. They will only spread their ideas of Aryan dominance through the *Ramayana* and *Mahabharata*. What about us Dravidians? Along with power, are we to surrender pride and dignity?

TANTRIC: I understand how you feel.

DRISHTI: So, we must find a way to get rid of this child. That interfering pandit has become his guardian and may even earn the protection of the King.

TANTRIC: How did he convince him?

DRISHTI: With argument and debate. No one can dispute well enough with the pandit. He's a master of words.

TANTRIC: Then do not tackle him with words. Break his spirit with deeds.

DRISHTI: But what if I can't break him?
TANTRIC: Then find a rich man to secure your future. The wealthiest merchant of Kanchi—
DRISHTI: Oh, I know him well. That's my dear friend Abhira.
TANTRIC: — has named his little son Vajra. Take him under your wing. Have him trained in Vajramushti.
DRISHTI: Vajramushti? What is that?
TANTRIC: A killer's art so horrific that people buried it long ago. But I know a secret group that still practices it. It is the ancient art of close-fighting to the death. One hand grapples with the opponent, the other smashes his face in with a knuckleduster made of ivory or wood.
DRISHTI: [*Shudders*] Deadly.
TANTRIC: I have for you the ultimate weapon which only Vajra must use.

The Tantric produces a knuckleduster which has diamonds glittering on its points. He wears it on one hand and does a short, swift series of movements depicting an imaginary bout of Vajramushti. The diamonds sparkle and flash. Then he takes off the knuckleduster.

TANTRIC: Give it to him when the time is right.
DRISHTI: How will I know the time is right?
TANTRIC: When he returns from a long journey through the deserts of the north.
DRISHTI: [*Nods*] Ah.
TANTRIC: Till then keep it wrapped and sealed in this cloth protected with a yantra design.

The Tantric hands the wrapped knuckleduster to Drishti.

DRISHTI: Thank you, O Tantric. When I am king I shall build a stupa in your honour.
TANTRIC: Forget the stupa. Just a small palace will do.

Drishti laughs, salutes and leaves. The Tantric begins whirling while gurgling with laughter. The lights fade.

Scene 3

A metal grille set sideways, suggesting the ambience of a prison. Enter Drishti, Army Chief, carrying a few palm-leaf books and scrolls.

DRISHTI: Ho there! Bring me the Brahmin priest.

Two guards holding spears bring in Prajna in chains.

PRAJNA: [*Indignantly*] Why have I been arrested? Let me speak to His Majesty the King.
DRISHTI: [*To the men*] Unlock the chains. Leave him to me.

They unlock the chains and leave.

PRAJNA: I have done nothing wrong. Who are you?
DRISHTI: Drishtivisha Chola, Chief of Security and Chief of Army. Are these documents yours? They were found among your possessions.
PRAJNA: [*Glancing at them*] Yes! These are my notes and drawings.

DRISHTI: You do not deny they are yours?
PRAJNA: Why should I deny it?
DRISHTI: These are maps and plans about the city of Kanchipuram.
PRAJNA: I am a scholar on pilgrimage, studying the holy city of temples. There is an amazing variety here — Shaivite, Jain and Buddhist. Their layout and architecture interests me.
DRISHTI: You are a spy.
PRAJNA: [*Laughs*] Indeed.
DRISHTI: [*Surprised*] You acknowledge that? [*Suspiciously*] Who do you spy for?
PRAJNA: Myself and Saraswati.
DRISHTI: Who is Saraswati?
PRAJNA: The goddess of learning.
DRISHTI: [*A short laugh*] Ha, you are one of those clever jokers! Well, I am a blunt Buddhist. I have no time for mythic references that befog the mind. If you are a religious scholar, why were you going about the city asking secular questions?
PRAJNA: If asking secular questions makes a person a spy, then the Buddha was a spy.
DRISHTI: How can you say that?
PRAJNA: Did he not go about asking questions regarding birth, life and death? These are certainly secular matters because even an atheist goes through them.
DRISHTI: Hm. You are clever alright, perhaps even cunning. [*Sets the books and scrolls aside*] I can see how you tricked

the King into sparing the life of his third son, a boy whose evil *karma* killed his own mother in childbirth.

PRAJNA: It is stupid to blame the child for the death of his mother.

DRISHTI: [*Angry*] Are you calling me stupid?

PRAJNA: No. But such thinking is. See, they said the child would die but he draws breath easier now.

DRISHTI: The boy is unlucky, I tell you. He will bring misfortune to whoever is near him. Don't you wish to return home safe and sound?

PRAJNA: Oh, I long to go back to Mathura, to my own friends and relatives. But God has entrusted me this task and I must fulfill it.

DRISHTI: Even if it takes your entire life?

PRAJNA: [*Sighs*] I'm afraid so.

DRISHTI: The answer is simple.

PRAJNA: Yes?

DRISHTI: Tell the King that the boy should be brought up by a military man. That way the boy will grow up tough. In fact, I'll happily take charge of the child.

PRAJNA: Ah, I see. What you're really after is Prince Dharma. Why?

DRISHTI: Only for his own good.

PRAJNA: Then why didn't you save him when he was to be killed?

DRISHTI: Look, that child will only cause you trouble. He will always be considered a disgrace. The King doesn't even wish to set eyes on him. He'll never be strong enough to take blows, to fight. Why do you smile?

PRAJNA: You don't need strength for that, you need skill.

DRISHTI: [*Laughs*] I am a soldier, trained to be fierce in combat, and you — a mere priest — are telling me that you don't need to be strong. Look at me. Standing before you, I feel like a bull in front of a monkey.

PRAJNA: An apt description. The Pallavas are particularly fond of bulls.

DRISHTI: Are you mocking me? Well, I *am* like the Nandi bull. You would not be able to withstand one rush from me.

PRAJNA: What if I took three, using only your strength against yourself?

DRISHTI: [*Laughs*] Ridiculous! Let me call witnesses so I am not accused of ill-treating my prisoners. [*Calls out*] Guards, ho!

The two spear-bearing guards enter.

DRISHTI: [*To them*] Stand at ease. Do not intervene. [*To Prajna*] If you are still standing after even one of my charges, I will grant you whatever you want.

PRAJNA: [*Joining his palms in acknowledgement*] So be it.

DRISHTI: Prepare yourself.

PRAJNA: [*Exhales audibly*] I'm ready.

DRISHTI: What was that noise?

PRAJNA: The same breathing technique that I've taught the child. It taps into the *pranayama*. It comes from the practice of yoga.

DRISHTI: [*Laughs*] That won't help.

With a roar, he charges at Prajna who does not move till the last split-second. Then, with a flick of the wrist and a swirling motion, he throws Drishti who goes tumbling over. The two guards move towards Prajna but Drishti rises and waves them back. Then he attacks again, but differently, and is swung away, differently. Prajna remains calm and composed. Drishti is furious. Prajna turns away as though bemused.

DRISHTI: You dare turn your back on me as if I were a plaything! That is a mistake, scoundrel!

Prajna turns around. Drishti retreats a few paces. Then, with a roar, he runs at Prajna with his fist held out like a battering-ram. On impact, he crumples at the knees and holds up an open hand in agony. He moans in pain. The two guards move quickly to help him up.

PRAJNA: [*Sympathetically*] Let me see. [*Does*] I think you've broken your wrist.
DRISHTI: Ohhh. You are a strange opponent.
PRAJNA: There are no opponents, only partners in the process of learning.
DRISHTI: This is terrible. I am humiliated!
PRAJNA: [*Calmly*] No, you have learnt something. To keep your wrist straight when you attack. Now, for your next strike at me, since your wrist is injured, you will have to use your other hand.
DRISHTI: [*Considers his hands*] I ... I have no wish to damage the other hand too.

PRAJNA: Then you may wield a stick.
DRISHTI: What? Did you say I could use a stick?
PRAJNA: [*Nods*] A wooden staff. Or, if you prefer it an iron rod.
DRISHTI: I don't believe it.
PRAJNA: Do it and you will believe it.

With his good hand, Drishti grabs hold of a spear from one of the guards, turns it and uses the wooden shaft, swinging it against Prajna's stomach. The shaft breaks in two. He looks at the piece in his hand in consternation. Throwing it down, he grabs the second guard's spear and quickly turns on Prajna with a shout.

DRISHTI: Ha!

He jabs forward with the spear, thrusting it at Prajna's face. Prajna drops into a low, straddle-legged stance, crosses his wrists and pushing up, holds the shaft and twists the spear fluently out of Drishti's grasp. Then, in one swift motion, he whirls round, strikes Dhrishti on the shoulder with the shaft so that, caught off-balance, Drishti falls. Prajna holds the point of the spear at Drishti's chest. The two guards seem uncertain. Prajna glances at them.

PRAJNA: [*To the guards*] Stay where you are!
DRISHTI: I ... I lost my temper.
PRAJNA: That is the last thing you can afford to lose when you fight. Get up.
DRISHTI: You have survived my blows. That *is* amazing! I promised to grant you what you want, so what will it be?

PRAJNA: Leave Dharma in peace till he is a grown man, then you may pit him against the best in the country, in unarmed combat — to the very death, if you wish.

DRISHTI: [*Astounded*] Granted. Granted. [*Then controlling his delight*] Of course, I have no reason to wish him ill. But should you want to test the training you give him, I shall be happy to oblige, by finding the strongest antagonist possible for him. Anything else?

PRAJNA: The greatest intellectual wave sweeping the world these days is Buddhist learning. The best universities are now Buddhist — Kashmir, Kanchi and the new one coming up at Nalanda. While Dharma is still a child and growing, I would like to devote some of my time to study. I would like to join the university of Kanchi.

DRISHTI: No problem. I thought you would ask for something more than that. [*Proudly*] When the Chief of Army, a Buddhist, recommends you, you will be seated amongst the most brilliant monks and scholars and princes.

PRAJNA: Thank you. But I will also require a loan. I will need money for four years of university fees, books, clothes—

DRISHTI: You know, you're quite funny. All this and all you want is a scholarship stipend!

PRAJNA: Just ten gold coins, which I shall work to repay when I can.

DRISHTI: You shall have twenty.

PRAJNA: That will be harder to repay.

DRISHTI: I have no intention of making things easy for you. I want you in my power. The more indebted you are to me, the happier I shall be.

Prajna laughs and flings the spear aside.

PRAJNA: Have I your permission to leave?
DRISHTI: Of course. The money will be delivered to your chambers within the hour. As for the university, they will be expecting you at the College of Buddhist Studies tomorrow morning.

Prajna bows, picks up his palm-leaf books and scrolls, and starts to leave. The two guards look at each other, whisper together and move towards him. He turns alertly to them. They withdraw, somewhat afraid. He turns again to leave. They glance at each other and move forward. He turns to them.

GUARD 1: [*Hesitantly*] We wondered, sir, if you ever start training people in the art of fighting, may we join and learn from you?

*With a gentle smile, Prajna bows affirmatively **and** leaves.*

Scene 4

A crowd clustered in a group watching the wrestling taking place offstage. The group moves backwards onto the stage with the cohesion of a hydra, its body swaying as one, its many heads sometimes at variance — sometimes in consonance with each other.

ONE: See, I told you he'd tear him apart!
TWO: I wouldn't give a copper coin for the prince's chances.

ONE: They should've let him die at birth.
THREE: Oh look! He's been thrown again. He's running! He's running!

General laughter.

ONE: Like a scared rat!
THREE: Yanked back by his tail. [*Laughs*]
TWO: That's his loin-cloth, you fool. Pulled him back by his — Oh!

A general groan.

THREE: Too much, too much. He can't even breathe.
TWO: Flat on his arse, poor fellow.
ONE: No wonder the King would rather have seen him dead.
FOUR: You bastards! Have you no loyalty? That's Prince Dharma, after all.
ONE: Prince or no prince he shouldn't be in the pit if he can't wrestle.
THREE: Yeah! He should wear bangles.
TWO: Hey, watch out, he's running this way!
FOUR: [*Shocked*] He's scrambling to get away.
THREE: Block him off! Block him off!
ONE: Yaah, he must fight.
TWO: [*Cupping hand to mouth*] Coward!
ONE: Shame!
TWO: Shame!
THREE: Shame!
FOUR: Traitor!

The crowd scatters and regroups to one side as Prince Dharma, begrimed and embattled, wearing a gold headband and diamond-stud earrings, is flung — hurtling and falling — onto the stage.

A man in a green headband follows, standing over him, clapping his own thighs in preparation for the next encounter.

Vajra, a well-built young man in a red headband, and Drishti, in a yellow headband, enter — watching.

Dharma gets up feebly and tries to fend off the wrestler who quickly picks him up and whirls him overhead and throws him down.

The crowd groans.

FOUR: [*Through cupped hands*] Come on, Prince Dharma, fight on, fight on!
ONE: [*To Four*] Arsehole, there's no fight left in the bugger, how can he fight on?

Dharma and the wrestler engage again. After a bit of scrambling and twisting and turning, the wrestler gets a lock on Dharma who begins to gasp for breath.

TWO: Where's the bloody referee?
ONE: What referee? This is a friendly bout.
VAJRA: [*Shakes his head*] This is murder.
DRISHTI: I know it's a disgrace but, you're too sensitive, Vajra.

VAJRA: I can't watch anymore.

They move away. The crowd becomes agitated, watching Dharma's vain efforts to free himself.

ONE: [*Shouts*] Hey, let him go. He's had enough!
TWO: You bastard, you're choking him to death!

Drishti leads Vajra forward by the elbow.

DRISHTI: You must learn to harden yourself. That man wins who has the killer instinct.
VAJRA: I know that, sir, but I can only fight when I am insulted. [*A small, rueful laugh*] Maybe that's why I'm happier on the street than in the gym. I enjoy a brawl that draws blood. Here everyone is protected by rules.
DRISHTI: [*Smiles*] You like fighting no-holds-barred, eh? That's a good sign. It shows we chose the right art for you. Vajramushti will make a champion of you among real men.
THREE: [*Shouts to wrestlers*] It's not fair! Pick on someone who can fight.
FOUR: The trouble with the prince is that he just won't give up.
TWO: He's more stupid than I thought.

In disgust, the wrestler flings Dharma down like a wet dishrag and leaves. Dharma remains on the ground, struggling to recover.

VAJRA: [*To Drishti*] Sir, you really must excuse me.
DRISHTI: Very well, my boy. Give your father my regards. Good luck!

Vajra goes. Drishti moves off in another direction. The crowd has been watching Dharma.

ONE: Serves him right.
TWO: Hey look, there's another bout starting there.
THREE: Come on!
ONE: Let's go.

As the crowd leaves, Four looks at Dharma, makes a spitting sound and shakes his head before going with the others.

Dharma sits up, takes the gold headband off and clenches it between his teeth as though to alleviate the pain and humiliation even while audibly struggling to regain his breath.

Prajna enters and looks at him.

For a while Dharma does not realize that he is not alone. When he does, he turns to Prajna and, in the process, is on his knees.

DHARMA: [*Abjectly*] Gurudev, what is my problem?
PRAJNA: [*Smiles*] You. You are your own greatest opponent. That man is master of the situation who is, first of all, master of himself.
DHARMA: All that is very well, Gurudev. You've told me that before.
PRAJNA: I've taught you everything I know — all the locks and holds and throws.
DHARMA: But I get breathless in the execution.
PRAJNA: I have taught you breathing techniques, special ways to focus all energy into great power.

DHARMA: But I need speed and effectiveness to combat the very power you have taught us all to use.

PRAJNA: Ah, I see what you mean! The very power I am asking you to use is the one that I have taught all the others to use. So, how can you win against that?

DHARMA: Exactly. By the time, I think of a counter, I am already down.

PRAJNA: Thought is too slow.

DHARMA: Is there anything faster?

PRAJNA: [*Nods*] Conditioned reflex. That's where training tells.

DHARMA: But the wrestler's art is itself too slow. I dread the time it takes to get a grip and make the other man trip. In the world of words, it would be like looking for a quick definition but getting dragged into a lengthy debate. So I must find something that is faster than thought, faster than breath. Something that will enable me to win before the very same locks and holds and throws are used against me.

PRAJNA: [*Laughs*] If you ever find that you will be a white rock in the mist, a black rock in the dark.

DHARMA: Where can I find the answer?

PRAJNA: As always, study life but look within. I personally think what you are seeking is impossible. But then I am only me. It never even occurred to me to defeat the very skills I practice. [*Holds out his hand*] Come, you need to bathe and refresh yourself.

DHARMA: [*Gets up*] Do you think my search for an alternative is a coward's way out of a dilemma? I feel I am too weak to wrestle.

PRAJNA: You are no coward. But you may be a fool looking for an answer that does not exist.

They begin walking away.

DHARMA: Do you know everything that exists?

PRAJNA: [*Stops*] No. But if you ever find a way of unarmed combat that is faster than thought, faster than breath, place before me a white stone and a black, and I shall know you have reached the threshold of invincibility. [*Smiles*] Then, of course, I shall put you to the test.

They go.

Scene 5

Sangha — an attractive, somewhat mature young woman — comes down the street, carrying a cane basket in one hand. Behind her comes Vajra, in the red headband, as though he wished to talk to her but dare not. Twice, she stops, frowns and looks at him. He stops awkwardly, and pretends he is invisible. The third time, she stops, turns and confronts him.

SANGHA: Sir, are you following me?
VAJRA: No. That is, yes. I mean—
SANGHA: How dare you!
VAJRA: [*Overcome*] Oh, absolutely.

SANGHA: In broad daylight. Down a public street.
VAJRA: You're Sanghameeta, daughter of General Drishtivisha Chola—
SANGHA: Look, mister, I know who I am.
VAJRA: I am Vajrasena, son of—
SANGHA: [*Nods*] Son of Aditya Abhira, the richest merchant in Kanchi.
VAJRA: You know who *I* am?
SANGHA: Do I look like an idiot to you, mister?
VAJRA: No, no, no. And please call me Vajra. Mister sounds terribly formal. I'm so glad you know who I—
SANGHA: The elite of a city always know everything about each other and then pretend to discover it all. I know my father takes a great interest in you. He's having you trained in some kind of sport. Right? And you're in love with me.
VAJRA: [*Opens his mouth to protest then collapses into the truth*] Yes.
SANGHA: Well, there's no hope for you.
VAJRA: That's what your father said.
SANGHA: My father? He has no business to interfere in my life!
VAJRA: Exactly what I thought. He said there was no hope for me as long as Prince Dharma was alive. He said you were besotted with the prince. How could you be? He's such a ... a ... wimp.
SANGHA: What?

VAJRA: We've just been to see him fight. He's like a wet dishrag. There's no spirit in him. He couldn't defend himself. He was thrashed mercilessly.

SANGHA: Oh my God, I must go to him.

VAJRA: Wait. The reason I was following you is that I wanted to speak to you—

SANGHA: [*Turning to go*] We have spoken.

VAJRA: [*Catches her arm*] I'm going away for four years. Leading a trade delegation to Persia. Give me some token to remember you by.

SANGHA: Are you insane? [*Brushes his hand off*] I know they call you Fighter-cock Vajrasena—

VAJRA: [*Proudly*] I *am* the best fighter in the kingdom of Kanchi.

SANGHA: You've bloodied every street for that renown. I used to wonder what made you so angry. But now I see that you are also completely mad.

VAJRA: Yes I am, but it's love for *you* that's driven me to it. I'm not like Prince Dharma who cares for nothing except his own spiritual development. Do you know what he is thrilled by right now? That he has received a message from the ruling Patriarch of Buddhism who is coming from Magadha to Kanchi to see him! But, of course, I don't think he'll get here before we leave for Persia. Now, there you have that boring thinker and here you have me, a man of action—

SANGHA: Leave for Persia? What do you mean?

VAJRA: Didn't he tell you? Everyone knows. We've been

preparing for days. See he doesn't even care enough about you to tell you this.

SANGHA: They're trying to take him away from me!

VAJRA: Frankly, I don't know how I'm going to survive with such a dead duck around my neck for four years.

SANGHA: Four years? How will I live? Refuse to take him away.

VAJRA: I can't. He's a prince. That adds royal weight and dignity to the delegation. It will please the King of Persia and help our mission to succeed.

SANGHA: You fool, you're being used. I'm being used. We're all toys in the hands of these power-mongers.

As she begins to leave, he catches her arm and pulls her round.

VAJRA: A token is all I ask. Something to remember you by.

SANGHA: [*Freeing herself*] Don't touch me! [*She slaps him*] There's your token! [*She storms off*]

VAJRA: [*Touching his cheek. Softly*] I love the fire in you.

Scene 6

A bruised and battered Prince Dharma seated cross legged in meditation. Sangha enters in a huff.

SANGHA: Imagine the cheek of that Vajrasena fellow, following me around like a dog!

There's no response from Prince Dharma who continues meditating. She puts her bag down.

SANGHA: Can you imagine, in broad daylight...in the middle of the street...telling me he loves me [*Glances at Dharma. No response*] and then he touches me... [*No response*] ... tries to turn me against you... Troublemaker! [*Sits down*] He's like that. Full of himself... a show-off.

Prince Dharma sighs, rubs his hands together and places the heels of the palms over his eyes.

SANGHA: Didn't you hear me?

DHARMA: Of course. In meditation, you hear everything. You hear ants talking, the fire singing. All your perceptions are heightened. But you are calm, beyond all feeling.

SANGHA: Beyond feeling... even jealousy?

DHARMA: [*Smiles*] Oh, come now, Sanghameeta, don't I have turmoil enough? Don't provoke me into an emotion that is unnecessary.

SANGH: You are right. I am stupid.

DHARMA: No, no, no. Please understand. The senses play games with our feelings making it difficult to think clearly.

SANGHA: [*Playfully*] Then you must teach me to think clearly. Or shall I have to join the charmed circle of Prajna disciples to learn from the 'Great Master' himself?

DHARMA: Don't be sarcastic. You're always trying to make fun of him. He's a brilliant teacher. No one can match him in logic.

SANGHA: Oh, all that clap and answer business [*She*

ACT ONE | 27

demonstrates] is ridiculous! As if being forced to think quickly makes you think better.

DHARMA: [*Shrugs*] Nobody can beat him in an argument.

SANGHA: I can.

DHARMA: [*Laughs*] one day you might have to prove that.

SANGHA: [*Confidently*] Any day. [*Examining him*] God, you're injured! Bruised all over. Oh, my sweet Prince. Come. Come over here. [*Leads him by the hand to the basket*] See, I've brought you herbs, ointments and a brew that will delight you. It invigorates the body and the mind.

He sits casually at her feet. She begins to apply balms and lotions to his bruises. A pause. She pours a liquid into a bowl and he sips it.

DHARMA: Hm. This bitter-sweet drink is most refreshing. What is it?

SANGHA: A brew that helps keeps you awake. I read about it in Sushruta's treatise on herbs and plants. It's made from the tender leaves of the Camellia plant. It's called 'cha'.

DHARMA: I like it. It's quite wonderful how you find for me the very things I need.

She takes out a palm-leaf manuscript and places it in his hands. He looks at the title then opens it at random here and there. Suddenly he stops and looks up at her then reads from the book.

DHARMA: My God, this is about the secret art of Marma Adi! [*Reads*] "There are 107 points in the human body that can lead to injury, some to unconsciousness, a few even to death." [*Looks at her*] Where did you get this?

SANGHA: I'm afraid I can't tell you. You yourself said it's a secret art.

DHARMA: But you must tell me who practices it. I want to meet this person. Who is he?

SANGHA: A ... a relative. A distant relative. A cousin who lives ... very far away. [*Glances at the book*] He's an expert in ... Marma Yoga. He knows about nerve-endings and the nervous system of the body. He can ... he can [*Thinks*] make a man unconscious with a touch and revive him with a blow.

DHARMA: I shall read this and all that you've brought me before. And then I should like to meet this relative of yours, this cousin. With such dangerous possibilities, you need to learn to be careful.

SANGHA: But ... but he lives far away from here, somewhere near the west coast. He comes and goes at will. He would be impossible to find.

DHARMA: What a pity! [*Excitedly*] I've heard it said that knowledge of this art is passed on by practitioners to only one person in their lifetime — someone they can trust. In the wrong hands it could be misused. [*Thinks*] An amazing possibility has just occurred to me Sangha! If this knowledge is carefully used and linked to a speedy and precise system of delivery then one man can be invincible against many. I must meet this relative of yours. Perhaps your father can put me in touch with him.

SANGHA: [*Quickly*] He doesn't know him. Don't ever mention this book to him. He has no link with him.
DHARMA: But I thought he was your cousin?
SANGHA: On my mother's side. My father never bothered with that side of the family. And my mother's dead. So the matter is sealed.
DHARMA: What do you mean 'sealed'?
SANGHA: Well, we certainly can't find him before you go to Persia. *Aai yai yo*, I'm devastated to hear you're off again!
DHARMA: [*Sighs*] Ah yes, Prajna insists. He says my education would not be complete without a visit to the Mahayana monasteries of the north.
SANGHA: But why Persia?
DHARMA: It's to do with trade. The Romans complain that the goods we send by sea land on the Arab coast of Africa. The Arabs carry the goods to Europe and raise the price a few hundred times. So Prajna suggested we open our own land-route via Persia.
SANGHA: Ah, Prajna again! Has he been dealing with the Romans? Filling his pockets with drachmas?
DHARMA: [*Shocked*] Sangha! You can't talk of Prajna like that. The idea of a land route is good for Kanchi. We leave at dawn tomorrow.
SANGHA: Tomorrow? So quickly? Hunh! Prajna is a crafty old —
DHARMA: I've told you before, don't speak ill of my guru! [*Calls out*] Ho, Tambi! Come in. I'm waiting for you. Where are you? Tambi!

SANGHA: You're annoyed. You want me to leave?
DHARMA: Take your own time. This is the hour I devote to Kallaripayatu practice.

Tambi, a lithe young man, enters and joins his palms in greeting. Dharma nods.

SANGHA: Dharma, you can't practice anything in your condition. You're injured. [*To Tambi*] He's not well.
DHARMA: You're not my nursemaid.
SANGHA: What?
DHARMA: [*To Tambi*] Begin. [*Then relents*] She's right. I'm not in good shape today. Just show me some stances and blocks.
TAMBI: As always, we must begin first with the *surya namaskar*.

He does. Meanwhile;

SANGHA: [*To Dharma*] one day you'll appreciate all I do for you.
DHARMA: I do. It's just that sometimes the blunt way you speak is so … upsetting.
SANGHA: I can't help that, *enh?* I am what I am. Not like you genteel Pallava Brahmins.
DHARMA: [*Stung*] Sangha!
TAMBI: And now, the crocodile walk and other warm up exercises.

He does them.

SANGHA: [*To Dharma*] See, I did it again. I've irritated you.
DHARMA: You hurt me. I must learn to be … non-attached.

TAMBI: Now the kicks.

He demonstrates. Dharma watches pensively. Tambi does a repertoire of movements.

SANGHA: Miss me while you're away. I'll be waiting to greet you when you return. [*Going, stops*] Vajra says you don't care about leaving me here. He says you're only concerned that you'll miss meeting the old Patriarch of Buddhism when he visits Kanchi.

DHARMA: [*With great animation*] Oh, how I wish I could stay back for that!

SANGHA: Well, don't worry. He'll be here when you return. I've heard he wants to set up a stupa and vihara in Kanchi for his great China mission. All that will take him more than five years to build.

DHARMA: Sangha, will you do me a favour?

SANGHA: Of course. You only have to ask.

DHARMA: Meet him on my behalf and tell him, "I have thought deeply on the teachings of the Buddha and would like to follow that path of wisdom."

She looks at him in stunned delight. The lights fade.

Scene 7

A room in Drishti's house with a low desk and traditional writing materials. To one side is a huge blackboard of slate with a variety of arrowheads drawn in chalk. Drishti is frantically searching the room with increasing exasperation. Sangha enters.

SANGHA: Appa!
DRISHTI: [*Spins round*] Oh God! You gave me a start. You mustn't barge in like that without warning. You know this is my study and I am in the middle of —
SANGHA: [*Delightedly*] Prince Dharma has decided to become a Buddhist!
DRISHTI: What?
SANGHA: Isn't it marvellous?
DRISHTI: No! It's disastrous.
SANGHA: How can you say that, Appa? It's the greatest thing that could have happened. Now, maybe, he can marry me. [*Gleefully*] It'll be one Buddhist with another!
DRISHTI: What're you talking about, child? Buddhist or no, he is a Pallava and a prince. An Aryan. You are Dravidian. At worst he'll treat you like a courtesan, at best like a concubine. Till today the Pallavas issue all their edicts in Sanskrit or Prakrit or Pali but never in Tamil. You may gain favour with them but you will never enter the bloodstream of the royal house. [*More quietly*] I feel depressed sometimes that I cannot overthrow them. Even my soldiers love them. It is as if I had a body that did not obey the brain. I am paralyzed.
SANGHA: [*Going to him. Teasingly*] Oh my dear father, you are a patriot without a people, a leader without a following. But perhaps I can breach that problem by providing the royal house with its first Tamil princess. Or perhaps even its first Tamil queen.
DRISHTI: Oh! You are clever, my little Sangha. You know

how to beguile me with impossible dreams. But no, there's no other way for us Cholas. It's humiliating to serve these foreigners who rule our land. We have to dislodge them before they become too popular. [*Gloomily*] Now the news that one of the princes has become Buddhist will endear them even further to the vast Buddhist population.

SANGHA: But that's wonderful!

DRISHTI: Come here, my daughter, listen to me. [*Wipes the blackboard clean, then draws with chalk*] These Pallavas who control the entire southern peninsula and all the trade to China, never intermarry with local people. Has it ever occurred to you that when it comes to marriage they send their princes all the way up north to Persia and the Hindu Shahi kingdoms for their brides? Remember, even Dharma's own mother was of Persian origin.

SANGHA: Oh my God, you frighten me, Appa! You mean, he'll never be allowed to marry me?

DRISHTI: Never. Can you not guess why His Majesty King Skanda jumped at the idea of sending Prince Dharma north?

SANGHA: In order to give Vajra's trade delegation the stamp of royal authority.

DRISHTI: Nonsense. The mark of the royal seal on a document would be enough. But along with the prince goes a caravan of elephants and camels laden with gifts.

SANGHA: [*With mounting anxiety*] The prince himself is only going because Prajna wants him to visit monasteries on the way.

DRISHTI: [*Smiles*] That's what he believes but we all know better.

SANGHA: Appa! [*Frantic*] I must go and warn him.

DRISHTI: There's no point. He'll probably be happy to go. Some of those Persian girls are lovely.

SANGHA: Appa, sometimes you really sicken me! Oh dear Lord Buddha, help me! I'm sure Dharma doesn't know of their plan.

She begins rushing out.

DRISHTI: Wait! [*She stops*] Remember to get my *marma adi shastra* back from him.

SANGHA: Appa, I don't know what you're talking about.

DRISHTI: I let you get away with certain things because you are my daughter, Sangha. But don't fool yourself that I don't know what is happening. I've seen you taking some priceless palm-leaf books from my library for Prince Dharma. I've never objected or stopped you. But the *marma adi shastra* is a dangerous work. and I want it back. I know you've stolen it...

SANGHA: Stolen?

DRISHTI: Taken, then. Taken without my knowledge and without my permission.

SANGHA: I'll see that it is returned after he reads it.

DRISHTI: [*Sternly*] No. Even I was not permitted to read it. That is why it was kept wrapped in a sacred yantra cloth which was stitched and sealed. It was here only for safekeeping.

He is glaring at her. She lowers her eyes and looks at the ground.

DRISHTI: And have you betrayed me completely? Have you told him of my links with the Tantric?

She looks up at him and slowly shakes her head.

DRISHTI: Never. Never. Never reveal that.

He sits down thoughtfully.

DRISHTI: Or my life will not be worth a nightingale's song.

She puts a hand on his shoulder.

SANGHA: I'll never betray you, Appa.

She goes. The lights fade.

Scene 8

Vajra and Dharma in warmer clothes shivering in a windy, snowy mountainous region. They are both travel-worn and unshaven.

VAJRA: [*Blowing on his fingers and rubbing his hands*] What do you mean, the next one? Why should we climb higher to the highest monastery? Each one is just like the other with snotty-nosed monks mumbling and grumbling prayers into their rancid butter. Aren't you sick of smelly yak's milk? I'm tired of the stink and the sleepless nights. And don't tell me that that one has better *thankas* and the other better *punkahs*. I frankly don't give a damn!

He waits for Dharma to speak. But Dharma seems to be self-absorbed.

VAJRA: Did you hear me? Hey, Prince Dharma, I'm talking to you. Down there on the plateau we've got a whole caravan of servants, with all the comforts of life. Musicians…dancers and strong liquor! We're supposed to be on our way to Persia in style. Then why are you dragging me up these slippery, treacherous paths to meet more of these weepy, old men? What are we doing up here?

DHARMA: [*Gently*] I am trying to come to terms with myself.

VAJRA: But why must I come to terms with you?

DHARMA: [*Smiles*] Indeed. I have no right to drag you about with me. You must do what is good for you. But, whenever I have left the caravan to visit a monastery, you have followed me.

VAJRA: Sometimes you make me quite angry. I follow you to protect you.

DHARMA: From whom? The only person I am in conflict with is myself.

VAJRA: Wonderful! High philosophy in the high mountains. Look, friend, sometimes one meets robbers and rogues in these remote places.

DHARMA: Then what would you do?

VAJRA: At the right opportunity, I would whip out [*He demonstrates*] my ivory knuckleduster and use my knowledge of Vajramushti.

DHARMA: Hm. Circular movements?

VAJRA: That's right.

DHARMA: Too slow compared to the speed and impact of the straight line.

VAJRA: What do you mean?

DHARMA: To climb this mountain, it's more comfortable to follow the path that goes round and round but if you went straight up it would be faster.

VAJRA: Another one of your great theories? Huh! Well, I believe in what I can do, not what I can't. I can't go straight up this mountain. And, frankly, I couldn't care less if you went straight down. I'm not Sangha.

DHARMA: Who?

VAJRA: Oh God, now he's lost his memory! Sangha is the girl who believes you love her.

DHARMA: Prajna would call that a fallacious assumption.

VAJRA: Help me, God. What shall I do with this man? [*Angrily, to Dharma*] It's not a phallic assumption!

DHARMA: [*Quietly*] Fallacious. I feel great affection for Sangha but I don't love her nor does she love me, though she may imagine she does.

VAJRA: Dharma, you exasperate and astound me.

DHARMA: But I also give you hope. Because I know you love her.

VAJRA: Yes, I do. I've always loved her. I'll do anything you ask if you persuade her to think kindly of me.

DHARMA: I will.

VAJRA: You will?

Dharma nods. Overwhelmed, Vajra embraces Dharma.

VAJRA: Thank you, my friend.

Dharma now walks away some distance thoughtfully, and turns round.

DHARMA: Then do *this* for *me*. Stop protecting me. Let me go about on my own. Sometimes I wish I were a monk so no one would bother where I wandered.

VAJRA: What about moving on to Persia?

DHARMA: You go and take the delegation with you. I'll join you later. There, or in Kanchi. I want to visit many places and see many things.

VAJRA: What about the sealed box your father gave you for the King of Persia?

DHARMA: You deliver it.

VAJRA: [*Going, stops*] Is there anything else I can do for you?

DHARMA: Take these diamond ear-studs. [*Taking them off*] Leave them with my attendant at the camp. I've always wanted to wear ordinary copper earrings. Now I can. [*Takes a pair out of a pocket and wears them.*]

Vajra bows then turns and leaves.

Scene 9

Prajna, pacing the floor, stops as Sangha comes in distraught, the tears running down her cheeks. Hanging from one arm is a garland of marigolds.

PRAJNA: Did you see him? Is he coming here?

Sangha nods, sits down and bursts into tears.

SANGHA: He's so different. Oh, Prajna, he's so changed. I couldn't even garland him. I forgot the *teeka*, the *aarati*...

PRAJNA: My child. Compose yourself. I suppose he'll go up to see the King first. Did you tell him that the Patriarch is coming here to meet him?

SANGHA: [*Nods*] He said it was a great honour. But, Prajna, he looks like a porter ... or one of these Chinese pilgrims ... carrying a load of books on his back. No one warned me. None of the attendants he sent back said anything. How was I to know he'd return looking like a beggar?

PRAJNA: Now, now, Sangha, a prince is still a prince no matter how he is dressed.

SANGHA: I wanted to embrace him, hug him, welcome him back. But I couldn't. I was so embarrassed.

PRAJNA: Embarrassed?

SANGHA: At the way *I* was dressed. I felt over-dressed, made-up, unreal.

PRAJNA: [*Smiles*] His simplicity shamed you.

SANGHA: Everyone just stood back and stared at him. Something has happened to him, Prajna. He is acting very strange. When I told him I would be here with you waiting to see him, he bent down, picked up two ordinary stones from the gravel and said, "Present these to my guru."

PRAJNA: [*Eagerly*] Two stones! Where are they?

SANGHA: Oh, I don't know. I threw them away.
PRAJNA: What?
SANGHA: [*Indignant*] Well, I wasn't going to obey a ridiculous command like that. Even from a prince! It hurts me to think he's going off his head. Imagine travelling all over and then presenting your guru two stones from your own backyard!
PRAJNA: [*Urgently*] What did the stones look like?
SANGHA: [*Shrugs*] Round, I think, and one was squarish, I suppose.
PRAJNA: No, no, what colour?
SANGHA: [*Thinks*] One was white. The other was black.

Prajna raises his hands in an ecstatic gesture of joy and thanksgiving.

PRAJNA: Ah! A white stone and a black!
SANGHA: Has the whole world gone mad?

Prajna is half-dancing, half-praying. He seems to be singing something like "Jai, Jai, Hari, Hari, Jai Jai!" Suddenly he turns to Sangha.

PRAJNA: Will you please tell your father that we are ready for his best fighter?
SANGHA: Indeed I will not! What kind of games are you playing, Prajna? You know as well as I do that the best wrestler in his stable is Vajra. And Vajra cannot control his emotions. The moment he loses his temper, he becomes a killer.

PRAJNA: Nevertheless, we are ready.
SANGHA: By 'we' you mean—?
PRAJNA: That's right. Prince Dharma.
SANGHA: No! Vajra is already furious with him and waiting to accost him. Ever since Vajra returned from Persia, he's been talking of avenging the wrong that Dharma did him. I've had to use all my charms to pacify him.
PRAJNA: I know. So tell him that Dharma is here and at his mercy.
SANGHA: Oh, you men are brutes! I refuse to be a part of this.

Prince Dharma enters. He is bearded and clad quite simply. On his back he carries, mountain-porter-style, a stack of scrolls and manuscripts. He joins his palms and bows to Prajnaratna, then touches his feet.

DHARMA: Gurudev Prajna, *pranam!*
PRAJNA: Welcome home, Dharma. Here, let me look at you. There's colour in your cheeks. The mountain air has done you good. But ... you're still underweight. Let me see. Ah, some muscle at last on your arms. Altogether, there's been some improvement in physique.
DHARMA: [*Setting down his load and unpacking it*] And in the mind, Gurudev. Wait till I tell you of all the people I met, the discussions we had, the points that were raised about space, time, the nature of the universe, matter, duality and non-duality —
PRAJNA: Slowly, slowly, in due course.

DHARMA: Oh, it was so exhilarating!

PRAJNA: [*Pointedly*] Sanghameeta has a garland of marigolds for you.

SANGHA: Ah, yes, I almost forgot again! [*She garlands him*]

DHARMA: I have much to tell you too, Sangha. [*To Prajna*] And I brought you the palm-leaf books you wanted — the Lankaavatara and the Mahayana texts.

SANGHA: [*To herself*] I don't know why I'm suddenly shy!

PRAJNA: [*To Dharma*] I shall look at the books by and by. But, tell me, are you ready for your meeting with the Patriarch? He should be here any moment.

DHARMA: I'm very keen to meet him. And he knows that, thanks to you, Sangha.

Vajra barges in. He is livid. Sangha tries to hold him back.

SANGHA: Please. No.

He pushes her aside.

VAJRA: There you are, you scoundrel Dharma! Sneaking back to Kanchi, thinking you are safe in the palace. I'm going to teach you a lesson—

As he attacks Dharma, Prajna intervenes and blocks him off.

PRAJNA: [*To Vajra*] Stop! Not here. In the sparring pit. If you injure the prince here, the king will have you executed.

VAJRA: [*To Dharma*] You're going to pay for this with your life.

DHARMA: Why are you so angry?

VAJRA: Why am I angry? [*Looks at Sangha*] He asks why I am angry? [*To Dharma*] Haven't you been to see your father the king? Didn't he tell you?

DHARMA: We didn't talk about you. There were so many other matters.

VAJRA: Ha! I'm not worth bothering about, even after what you did to me?

DHARMA: I have no idea what you are talking about. What did I do to you?

VAJRA: You asked me to deliver the box of presents to the King of Persia.

DHARMA: Yes.

VAJRA: Inside the box, along with the presents, was a sealed letter from our King. It was read out to the entire court. It said, 'Please find for the bearer of these gifts a match of suitable standing from among the ladies of your court.'

DHARMA: Good heavens, it was a trap meant for me!

VAJRA: But you made me the victim of it. What're you smiling for? What're you laughing about?

DHARMA: It is quite funny.

VAJRA: It's not funny. I'm now engaged to the richest woman in Persia.

DHARMA: Congratulations!

VAJRA: She is squint-eyed, buck-toothed, addicted to opium and laughs like a hyena.

DHARMA: Sorry. Condolences.

VAJRA: You did this to me deliberately.

DHARMA: I did not.
VAJRA: Yes, you did. You knew of this plan. So you quietly slipped away to the monasteries and let me get trapped. Because you wanted to deprive me of Sanghameeta in spite of what you said.
DHARMA: What? That's not true.
VAJRA: Isn't it? Well we'll see. In the sparring pit at the tenth hour.

Vajra turns on his heel and leaves.

PRAJNA: What do you say, Dharma?
DHARMA: But, Gurudev, he's an experienced fighter.
PRAJNA: And you are a trained one.
DHARMA: My training is not over.
PRAJNA: It is never over. But you sent me the stones.
DHARMA: That is so. [*To Vajra*] Very well. As you wish.

Sangha looks dismayed. At that very moment two princes — Nandivarman and Shivavarman — in royal regalia enter.

NANDI: Ah, there you are, you wanderer!

He strides towards Dharma who bends to touch his feet. Nandi embraces him.

DHARMA: Nandivarman! It's wonderful to see you.
NANDI: Welcome home, dear brother.

Shivavarman has hung back slightly. Dharma moves to touch his feet.

ACT ONE | 45

SHIVA: God, you're a sight! You'd better change before the Patriarch gets here.

They embrace. Dharma laughs.

DHARMA: O Shivavarman, fastidious as ever! I'm afraid he'll have to see me as I am. I can already hear him coming.

The sound of drums and bhikshus chanting grows louder, nearer. The two princes greet Prajnaratna and Sangha with smiles and joined palms. They respond similarly. The Patriarch enters. He's a jovial, giggly old man with kind, smiling eyes. He first pranams Prajnaratna then, turning to the three princes and Sangha, he raises his hand in blessing. They bow and join their palms.

PATRIARCH: [*To Sangha*] How are you, my dear? It's always a joy to see you. Would you please fetch from my attendants outside the tray covered with a silken cloth?

SANGHA: Of course, Your Holiness.

She goes out.

PATRIARCH: I am here for a specific purpose. [*Giggles*] So I shall come straight to the point.

Sangha comes in with the tray.

PATRIARCH: King Skandavarman has been most generous with me.

He giggles and lifts the cover of the tray displaying a heap of precious jewellery on it.

SANGHA: Oh my goodness!
PATRIARCH: Persons of the royal household are well-acquainted with precious ornaments and therefore it interests me to ask what value they place upon it. I address myself to the three princes. What, in your opinion, is more valuable than this jewellery?
NANDI: May I examine it?
PATRIARCH: Of course.

He gestures to Sangha to show it to each of the princes. She takes the tray round.

NANDI: [*Impressed*] There's a fortune here. It would certainly help build a couple of ships for your China mission.
PATRIARCH: [*Giggles*] Oh yes, I'd be very interested in anything that furthers my China project.
PRAJNA: Hm. So that's what it's all about!
PATRIARCH: Of course, my dear friend. I want a valuation that will help me use these precious items so that I get more than their value.
PRAJNA: Very sensible. And crafty.
PATRIARCH: [*Giggles*] Well, gentlemen?
NANDI: I have a ruby the size of my fist. That, I think, would be more precious than all this.
PATRIARCH: [*Nods*] Prince Shivavarman?
SHIVA: [*Taking a deep breath*] Five of my houses would together out-value these.
PATRIACH: Very well. Prince Dharmavarman?
DHARMA: [*Shakes his head*] I'm afraid I'm no good at this. To me, my books [*Points to the pile*] are more precious.

Sangha and the two princes laugh. Prajna looks at the Patriarch and smiles.

NANDI: Good God, Dharma, your travels have addled you! You could buy those books a million times over with the wealth on this tray.

SHIVA: Easy to have copies made. And they're pretty tattered anyway.

DHARMA: [*Looking down, sighs*] I'm sorry but that's how I feel.

PATRIARCH: And why do you feel that?

DHARMA: Because the knowledge in these books is priceless.

The Patriarch goes to Dharma and places a hand on his head.

PATRIARCH: My son.

A moment's pause. The Patriarch walks a few steps then turns thoughtfully.

PATRIARCH: The wisdom of that answer has moved me deeply. [*To Prince Nandi and Prince Shiva*] Thank you, my boys, for giving me so much of your time.

Prince Nandi and Prince Shiva pranam him and leave.

PATRIARCH: [*To Dharma*] You have the right values. Someone who is a jewel among teachers has taught you. I want to give credit where it is due.

DHARMA: Your Holiness, my guru is undoubtedly the source of all my learning.

PRAJNA: You are embarrassing me now, you two.
PATRIARCH: *Prajna* means wisdom and *ratna* means jewel. If he is the jewel of wisdom, then what am I? My name is Prajnatara.
PRAJNA: *Tara* means celestial being. [*Indicating the Patriarch wrily*] There stands the wisdom of the celestial being. In other words, it's time my protégé moved from precious earthly wisdom to heavenly wisdom.
PATRIARCH: [*Gently*] It's better for his spiritual development.
PRAJNA: Of course. [*Moves away*] I knew it would come to this some day. I tried to prepare myself.
PATRIARCH: Well, if it will help ease the parting, let me remind you of what you said during our discussions. You said you longed one day to go back to Mathura with a sense of achievement. What you have achieved has far greater value to me than these jewels. I give them to you in return for this one.

The Patriarch takes the tray from Sangha and himself carries it to Prajna who does not touch it. The Patriarch then places it at Prajna's feet.

PRAJNA: That's very generous of you. I would have let him go anyway. What do you plan for him?
PATRIARCH: After due instruction and preparation — China.
SANGHA: [*Shocked*] China!
DHARMA: Then I would like to go as a monk.
SANGHA: What?

PATRIARCH: The life of a monk is rigorous, requiring great discipline.

DHARMA: I have that.

PATRIARCH: Then ... [*Giggles and indicates Prajnaratna and himself*] ... earthly wisdom and heavenly wisdom must meet this evening to agree on a major decision which I shall convey to you tomorrow. Meanwhile, I suggest you work out what you may require for the success of your mission in China. Take with you a small group of persons with such knowledge and skill as may help the people of that land.

DHARMA: I would certainly require a skilled healer. [*To Sangha*] Your cousin. The one you said had become a monk. The man who is practiced in the art of *marma adi*. I must take him along. Such a person would be of great assistance with his herbal medications, massages and ability to mend bones.

PATRIARCH: Of course, she will get hold of this relative for you. If he is a monk I can order him to go as part of your group. [*To Sangha*] Shall I speak to your father about it?

SANGHA: No, no. No need to do that. I'll find a way to get hold of him.

PATRIARCH: Good. [*Giggles*]

The lights fade.

Scene 10

Drishti and Sangha at home in mid-argument.

DRISHTI: What are you suggesting?
SANGHA: That we do send my cousin Vellu with him.
DRISHTI: Vellu? What Vellu? Who is Vellu?
SANGHA: *Aai yai yo,* you know my cousin Vellu, three removed on Amma's side, the one whose eyes cannot bear the glare of daylight. He keeps his face hooded and hidden because his skin develops a rash in the sun.
DRISHTI: Hm. Curious. I don't remember him.
SANGHA: Appa, I'm ashamed of you!
DRISHTI: But remind me. Have I met him?
SANGHA: Never.
DRISHTI: Never? Not at any of the weddings and funerals?
SANGHA: He's an insignificant fellow.
DRISHTI: How tall?
SANGHA: About … about my height.
DRISHTI: Bearded?
SANGHA: Oh no, no. Absolutely smooth-skinned.
DRISHTI: But if his skin suffers from exposure to the sun, the thing to do would be to grow a beard and protect it.
SANGHA: He can't.
DRISHTI: What? Grow a beard? Why can't he grow a beard?
SANGHA: It … It is part of his condition.
DRISHTI: That's odd.
SANGHA: [*Quickly*] What's odd?

DRISHTI: That a man cannot grow a beard. Who *is* this strange fellow?

SANGHA: [*In tears*] Oh Appa, I must go with him.

DRISHTI: Go with Vellu? Where?

SANGHA: [*Crying*] To China.

DRISHTI: To Chi—! [*Surprised*] This fellow Vellu is also going to China?

SANGHA: [*Nods*] With Dharma.

DRISHTI: Who? Oh. Ah. Dharma.

SANGHA: I shall commit suicide.

DRISHTI: [*Gently*] Now, now, Sanghamma, let me understand this.

SANGHA: Oh Appa, it's so long since you called me Sanghamma! Remember, that's how you used to call me when I was a child? You'd say, 'Sanghamma, whatever you want I'll do for you.' I worshipped you then, Appa. I worshipped the ground you walked on.

DRISHTI: [*Coldly*] And now you worship the ground that Dharma walks on.

SANGHA: Appa!

DRISHTI: What are you trying to get out of me?

SANGHA: Permission.

DRISHTI: [*Stares at her*] Say that to me slowly and clearly so I follow what you are saying.

SANGHA: I want your permission to go to China.

DRISHTI: With a monk called Dharma? [*She nods*] You want to become a nun? [*She shakes her head*] Ah, I didn't think you were nun material.

SANGHA: [*With a flash of fire*] Don't push me, Appa. I would become a nun if—
DRISHTI: Too tough a discipline for you.
SANGHA: Ha! If I could be by my Dharma night and day, I would happily become a nun. As it is, I might become a monk.
DRISHTI: A monk? But you're a woman.
SANGHA: Vellu is a man. Dharma obviously wants such a *man* to be by him night and day. And Vellu is that man.
DRISHTI: So where is Vellu?
SANGHA: Standing before you.
DRISHTI: Impossible. You'll never be able to carry it off. [*Thinks*] No. No. No.
SANGHA: Otherwise I shall kill myself.
DRISHTI: [*Deeply distressed*] Oh my little Sangha, this man has obsessed you.
SANGHA: I want your help.
DRISHTI: It is not easy being a father. [*A slight pause*] Very well. I shall agree to your request on one condition.
SANGHA: Yes?
DRISHTI: That I depute a man to go along as a monk to look after you, should you need protection.
SANGHA: Oh alright, Appa, if you insist. And who is this man you are planning to send with me?
DRISHTI: Vajra.
SANGHA: Vajra?
DRISHTI: [*Nods*] Vajra.
SANGHA: But... but he won't want to become a monk.

DRISHTI: When my men go on assignment they don't become what they say they are. They just pretend to be that as a cover. Anyway, he would love to go. First, because of you, and also to free himself from his Persian fiancée. Morever, his family has property in China. But, of course, all this depends on the fight tomorrow. I doubt Dharma will survive that.

SANGHA: Surely you don't think he's going to fight? He can say he's becoming a monk. Monks don't fight.

DRISHTI: They do from now. He'll be the first fighting monk. He won't try and slip out of it. He's a Pallava. They never go back on their word.

The lights fade.

Scene 11

Lights, music and sound-effects enhance the impact of the fight that is taking place centrestage between Vajra and Dharma. In a while it becomes evident that, despite some difficulty, Dharma is clearly winning. Then suddenly Vajra whips out the Diamond Fist and an entirely different scenario occurs. Dharma is hard put to it to avoid the diamond points. At last by a series of maneuvers, Dharma manages to make Vajra release the Diamond Fist.

For a brief moment, it seems as though Dharma may use the Diamond Fist against Vajra or even kill him with it but, quickly, he relents and slides the weapon away. Vajra is relieved and a momentary look of puzzlement crosses his face. He attempts to attack Dharma but, quite swiftly now, Dharma thrashes him till he falls unconscious.

Dhrishti signals to the stretcher bearers who come onstage and carry Vajra off. Prajna comes and stands beside Dharma.

PRAJNA: The winner is obviously Dharma!
DRISHTI: [*Enters*] But Vajra is not my best fighter. We had agreed that Dharma would take on the best.
DHARMA: [*To Prajna*] Agreed?
PRAJNA: [*Nods*] Many years ago. [*To Drishti*] Very well. If you have a better, bring him on.

Drishti signals and the Tantric walks on. Drishti grins and withdraws.

PRAJNA: Who is this?
DHARMA: It doesn't matter. Whoever he is, he is me, I am him.

Prajna looks at Dharma.

PRAJNA: Well said, my son. No anger. No fear. Beyond death. Totally calm.

The Tantric gives a gurgling laugh.

TANTRIC: If you are me and I am you, then neither can be faster than the other.
PRAJNA: He is faster than thought. The two stones told me that.
TANTRIC: But he cannot be faster than his own reflection.

I shall be that. [*Angrily*] Out of the pit, O Pandit, so we can settle this between us.

Prajna withdraws.

DHARMA: [*Calmly*] Whenever you are ready.
TANTRIC: Not yet. You've already warmed up with the earlier fight.

The Tantric begins to whirl on the spot and now he gives his gurgling laugh. Then he stops and does some quick, fluid movements for limbering up.

TANTRIC: Begin!

Dharma takes a one-legged stance with the front leg raised so that only the big toe touches the ground.

TANTRIC: Ah, the stance of the crane.

He adopts the same stance and gives a little flick with the front foot.

TANTRIC: Good for the sudden flick kick.

Dharma changes his stances, one after the other. In keeping with each, the Tantric comments. And replicates.

TANTRIC: The monkey. The tiger. The eagle. I see you are, like me, an observer of animals. I could show you some that you've never seen. But you are a silent fighter. You do not jump with a roar [*He leaps to the attack*]—or draw blood with a screech.

The Tantric makes a number of attempts to get through but Dharma fends him off each time.

TANTRIC: Alright, then. It looks like I shall have to wait to see what you can do. We'll be two snakes in a mirror.

The Tantric becomes a mirror-image of Dharma. Both fighters stay rooted to the spot. Neither blinks. When Dharma moves a hand so does the Tantric. When he smiles or frowns, so does the Tantric.

Dharma keeps his eyes on the Tantric but slowly begins to turn his head one way, so does the Tantric. Dharma quickly turns his back on the Tantric. The Tantric following the mirror pattern does the same. Dharma delivers a reverse roundhouse kick which strikes the Tantric on the neck throwing him off balance and down.

TANTRIC: So the mirror trick won't work! The snake became a donkey and kicked. I admit you are quick.

The Tantric spits on his hand and applies it to his neck and rises unhurt.

TANTRIC: I see now that you know something of the art I do. I could drop you, not with a kick or a blow, but with a touch. But you have not even let me touch you.

He lunges. Dharma blocks. He tries variously. Dharma deflects him each time, never allowing him to touch.

TANTRIC: This is not wrestling anymore. This is a skill of your own devising. You intrigue me. What will you do next?

Keeping his eyes on the Tantric, Dharma makes a gesture of throwing something up in the air. The Tantric looks up. Dharma jabs forward with the middle finger of the other hand, prodding the Tantric in his solar plexus. The Tantric begins gasping for air, drawing deep screeching breaths. He staggers about as though searching for help. Dharma stays alert and out of his reach.

TANTRIC: [*Gasping*] Help ... me.

Prajna and Drishti enter quickly.

DRISHTI: Good God, in the name of all that's holy, what is this?

PRAJNA: He only used one finger and look what's happened!

By slow degrees, the Tantric crumples to the floor.

PRAJNA: [*Suddenly*] Finish him off, Dharma! Kill him! This was a fight to the death. He would've killed you. [*Catching hold of Drishti*] You tell him, Drishti. Tell him your instructions to your fighter. He was to kill, was he not?

Drishti trembles and looks about helplessly, then turning to Dharma, nods.

DRISHTI: Yes, he would've killed you. By the rules, you may kill him.

Dharma makes a slow gesture indicating that they should move aside. They do. He stands over the prone Tantric, looks at him carefully, then he moves to his feet and, squatting down, takes up one foot, massages it and gives it a thump. The action is repeated with the other foot.

The Tantric sits up dazedly. He shakes his head as though to clear it. Seeing Dharma at his feet, he jumps up with a roar as though to attack.

DRISHTI: No, no, no. He saved you. He revived you. He gave you back your life!

The Tantric stops in amazement and looks at him. Drishti nods.

PRAJNA: He revived you when he could have killed you.

The Tantric is bewildered. Then he bows to Dharma.

TANTRIC: I shall remember.

Straightening up, he gurgles with laughter and whirls into the shadows and away.

PRAJNA: So, my friend, the announcement shall be made that the surprise champion of the Kingdom of Kanchi is none other than Prince Dharma.
DHARMA: Then add to it another surprise announcement and say that, as of today, I renounce the title of prince and embrace the calling of monk. Dedicating myself to spreading the message of the Buddha, I would like to be known not as Dharma but as Bodhidharma.
PRAJNA: Like someone at an auction pushed to bid higher, let me add surprise to surprise and announcement to

announcement. I received last night a visit from the Patriarch who told me what he had in store for my pupil.

DRISHTI: Ohhhh. I think I know what's coming. I have expected it much more than anyone else.

PRAJNA: You — a man who knows most secrets — would amaze me if you could reveal what had been kept locked away in the future. Do you know what the old man said? Can you guess?

DRISHTI: It makes my knees give way. He named, in your ear, the next great Patriarch of Buddhism.

PRAJNA: You astound me! He did, indeed. Declaring that the time had come for the faith to be led by a younger man with the energy and daring to forge the way in China, he gave me his mantle to place upon the shoulders of the one who will, from that moment, be his successor.

He gestures towards the wings and Tambi enters carrying the mantle folded upon an ancient begging bowl. He takes the mantle and drapes it round the shoulders of Bodhidharma. Then gives him the bowl.

PRAJNA: And the begging bowl that has come down to us from the days of the Buddha. It is yours. Bodhidharma — 28th Partriarch of Buddhism.

Drishti is so overwhelmed that he goes down on his knees and prostrates himself to Bodhidharma.

DRISHTI: My lord, my god on earth, my guide. [*Sitting back, still on his knees*] If there is ever anything I can do, anything at all, just say the word, Your Holiness.

BODHI: Rise, O Drishtivisha Chola. I intend to begin my journey by seeking an audience with the most powerful man on earth, His Exalted Majesty the Emperor of China. I wish to place before him the wonders of the knowledge and wisdom of this great country.

Drishti bows. The lights fade.

Act Two

Scene 1

The Emperor's court in China. The Emperor and courtiers.

EMPEROR: We should like to know something of this man who comes to us from the West before we meet him.

COURTIER 1: Sire, he is called Bodhidharma.

EMPEROR: Bo-ti Ta-Mo?

COURTIER 1: [*Bows*] Sire.

EMPEROR: You speak the language of the great Buddhist scriptures. Tell us what new ideas or knowledge he brings us from the West country, Yindu, the land of the Buddha.

COURTIER 1: From India, Sire, he brings the knowledge of meditation, of *dhyan*.

EMPEROR: Cha-an?

COURTIER 1: [*Bows*] Sire.

EMPEROR: This ... Tsa-an ... Tsen ... Zen?

COURTIER 1: Sire.

EMPEROR: What does it do?

COURTIER 1: *Dhyan* takes the mind beyond self and the self beyond mind.

EMPEROR: [*Impressed*] Yo. And how is this Zen ... this Tsa-an ... this Cha-an done?

COURTIER 1: There are many methods practiced by different persons —

EMPEROR: [*Impatiently*] But Ta-Mo, how does he do it?

COURTIER 1: He sits with his attention inward.

EMPEROR: So! He sits with eyes shut looking in?

COURTIER 1: With eyes open, staring out but looking in.

EMPEROR: Amazing. You have seen him do it?

COURTIER 1: Sire.

EMPEROR: What does he see?

The Courtier is confused and looks about uncertainly. Courtier 2, with a snigger on his face, bends towards the Emperor.

COURTIER 2: Your Exalted Majesty, he does not know.

EMPEROR: Do you? [*The Courtier is silenced. To Courtier 1*] Proceed. What else?

COURTIER 1: [*Bows. Then*] Bodhidharma was a prince of Kanchi. Now he wanders about as a monk with a stick over his shoulder and a pair of sandals hanging from it.

EMPEROR: Why?

COURTIER 1: To remind himself that he is no higher than the lowest.

EMPEROR: And yet he is the ruling Patriarch of Buddhism?

COURTIER 1: Sire.

EMPEROR: Strange, very strange. Now, from the teachings of the monk Kashyappa, who came to us earlier from Yindu, we know that Tsiangchi is a city of many temples. [*Benignly to his courtiers*] We shall build more. [*To Courtier 1*] Has he built any?

COURTIER 1: His father, King Skanda, has.

EMPEROR: Is King Sugandha more powerful than us?

COURTIER 1: No one is more powerful than you, Your Exalted Majesty.

EMPEROR: Yo. When this Bo-ti Ta-Mo is here before us, you will tell him of all the good works we have done.

COURTIER 1: [*Bows*] Sire, I will.

EMPEROR: You will tell him how all our power is used for deeds of merit.

COURTIER 1: He will understand the full extent of your greatness, Your Majesty.

EMPEROR: They say he has given up outer power for inner power and seeks outer strength from inner strength. What does that mean? What is inner power? How does he achieve that?

COURTIER 1: Through this *dhyan*, Your Majesty.

EMPEROR: This ... zen requires deep thought? Learning? Many ... scriptures? Vast knowledge?

COURTIER 1: He says ... [*Hesitates*] ... throw it away. He says there are intuitive leaps, between knowledge and wisdom, wisdom and enlightenment, and beyond.

EMPEROR: Ah. Curious. Call him in. Alone. Without the other monks. We would like to hear him expound on the works that have brought us merit.

Courtier 1 bows and signals to another who ushers Bodhidharma in. He bows politely, puts his stick and sandals down and waits while Courtier 1 speaks.

COURTIER 1: His Exalted Majesty, Emperor Wu-ti of the Liang Dynasty, has built eight hundred and twenty temples to the Buddha, five hundred and six resting places for pilgrims, eighteen hospitals for the sick, nine hundred li of new roads have been built lined with thousands of trees. He has venerated the scriptures and daily makes offerings for which hundreds of monks are obliged. He seeks to ask you how much merit he will have acquired through these good deeds?

BODHI: [*Stares at the Emperor. Then*] None.

At first the courtiers and the Emperor are not sure they have heard him correctly.

COURTIER 2: [*To Courtier 3*] Did he say none?

EMPEROR: [*To Courtier 1*] What did he say?

COURTIER 1: [*Trembling*] He said none, Your Majesty.

EMPEROR: None? [*Looks around*] None? [*To Courtier 1*] What can we expect, in return for our merit, in the after-life?

COURTIER 1: His Majesty desires to know what he can expect for his merit in the after-life.

BODHI: Nothing.

EMPEROR: Nothing! [*In a rage, glaring at Bodhidharma*] Who dares speak to me so?

The Courtier is about to explain to Bodhidharma but he stops him with a gesture.

BODHI: I do not know.
EMPEROR: [*Furious*] Who do you think you are?
BODHI: No one.

The Emperor rises and leaves stormily. There is consternation in the court.

COURTIER 1: [*To Bodhi, worriedly*] It would be best if you left the Kingdom. Quickly. His Majesty's anger will not be appeased without some action against you for such contradiction.
COURTIER 2: His anger is as well-known as his good deeds.

Bodhidharma bows and, putting stick and sandals over his shoulder, leaves. The lights fade.

Scene 2

An old Chinese woman seated by the bank of a river. Beside her are bundles of reeds for sale. Bodhidharma enters, bows politely to her while putting his stick and sandals down. He joins his palms in namaskar. She responds in the same way. He stands looking at the river.

WOMAN: The Yang-tse is swollen. It is not an easy river to cross. [*He looks at her and smiles. Then looks again anxiously at the river*] But the ferry boat will be here in two hours.

BODHI: That will be too late. [*He glances in the direction he had come*]

WOMAN: Ah, I see you speak Mandarin. You have studied our language?

BODHI: [*Nods*] A little, during the long voyage. I would like to learn more. To explain the teachings of the Buddha.

WOMAN: Good, good. And now you are desperate to cross beyond the reach of the Emperor. I have seen many who tried to swim across. They lost the very lives they were trying to save. Are you a strong swimmer?

BODHI: No. But I have a good sense of balance.

WOMAN: I don't know what you mean by that.

BODHI: Your reeds. How much for a bundle?

WOMAN: For two yuan you can have the lot. They're good to eat when they are green and good to burn when they are dry.

BODHI: But always, they float.

WOMAN: Ah yes! I see what you intend. But no one has tried it before. A bundle in the water would roll over and you would fall.

BODHI: Not if I have a good sense of balance.

WOMAN: But the river is rough.

BODHI: I am calm. [*Gives her a coin*] Here's one yuan. I'll take half the bundles.

He begins lashing the bundles together to make a raft. She helps him.

WOMAN: You must be that strange man. Ta-Mo from Yindu.

ACT TWO | 67

[*Laughs*] News travels faster than a man on the run. They say you insulted Emperor Wu-ti to his face.

BODHI: It was the truth.

WOMAN: [*Amused*] But you said it to his face. Others say it behind his back. You were right, Oh Holy Monk. What good is it to have ten temples on the bank when what you need is a bridge over the river or boats in which to cross?

BODHI: [*Smiles*] There, now, it is done. My raft of reeds is ready. All I need is an oar with which to row.

He ties a bundle of reeds to the end of his stick.

WOMAN: They say you also upset Hui K'o when he was lecturing in the marketplace.

BODHI: [*Busy at work. Smiles*] I didn't mean to.

WOMAN: Is it true that you distracted him so much that he threw his prayer-beads at you?

Bodhidharma reaches into a pocket and takes out a rosary of beads.

BODHI: [*Smiling*] Here, these are Hui K'o's prayer-beads. Return them to him when he comes. He will probably come with the Emperor's soldiers.

WOMAN: [*Laughs*] They think there is plenty of time before the ferry. [*Examining the rosary*] What lovely beads! Pure jade.

BODHI: Some Indian monks will come too, looking to join me. Tell them to take the ferry.

WOMAN: Where will you go?
BODHI: Wherever the spirit leads me.
WOMAN: [*Laughs*] I can do better than that. I can tell you where you will be safe from the brigands on the other side.
BODHI: Yes?
WOMAN: Climb up the mountain, beyond the temple of Shaolin, and you will find a cave in which no one lives.
BODHI: Perhaps I should seek shelter in the temple itself.
WOMAN: If the Abbot allows you. That Fang Chang is suspicious of any stranger. He wouldn't give the Buddha shelter if he came unannounced. Anyway, you would have no peace there. The brigands attack it all the time and take even the mats on which the monks sleep.
BODHI: Very well, I shall go on to the cave. Ask the Indian monks to meet me there. [*Joins his palms*] Thank you.

He slings the sandals, which are tied together, over his shoulder. Then carefully puts the raft in the water and lithely jumps on with the makeshift oar in his hands. He balances, enjoying the danger of it, then paddles with the oar while standing. The raft moves away and out of sight. She is peering after him and turns just as Hui K'o enters quickly with a couple of soldiers.

WOMAN: Ha, Hui K'o, how goes it with you?
HUI: You evil woman, you've helped him, haven't you? Where is he?
WOMAN: [*Points offstage*] There. Going across the river.
HUI: But how?

SOLDIER 1: There is no ferry boat yet.
SOLDIER 2: There, there, I can see him, standing on the water!
HUI: Standing on the water?
WOMAN: [*Laughs*] No, no. He is standing on the reeds.
HUI: [*To the soldiers*] Alright. We'll do the same. Let's catch him.

He grabs a bundle, chucks it in the water and jumps on. The soldiers do the same.

WOMAN: Hey, you haven't paid for the reeds!

They are teetering and tottering and trying to balance. They shout, exclaim, yell. And fall.

HUI: Help! Help!
SOLDIER 1: Give me your hand.
SOLDIER 2: Come on, pull him ashore.
HUI: Help! I'm drowning.

The soldiers manage to haul Hui K'o out of the river. The woman has been standing back.

SOLDIER 1: [*To the Woman*] You didn't help.
WOMAN: You didn't pay ... for my reeds.
SOLDIER 2: You were going to let us drown.
WOMAN: You were going away with my reeds.
HUI: [*Coughing and gasping*] That fellow Ta-Mo has gone off with my beads.
WOMAN: No, he hasn't. [*Holding them out*] He asked me to give them back to you.

HUI: Oh. [*Takes them*] Why?
WOMAN: I suppose he doesn't need beads to pray.
HUI: But these are jade.
WOMAN: Does that help you know the Buddha better?

The soldiers look at each other. Hui K'o looks down. A slight pause.

HUI: He is a good man. I will take the ferry to the other side and meet him.

The lights fade.

Scene 3

The gateway of the Shaolin Temple. Bodhidharma in conversation with Abbot Fang Chang while a couple of monks stand about listening.

FANG: In the circumstances, it would be very difficult for us to let you stay here. These are dangerous times. You must understand our position.
BODHI: I do. I had been warned. I shall move on.
FANG: How can we be sure you are who you say you are? Such an exalted person as Yindu's ruling Patriarch of Buddhism would be travelling with an entourage.
BODHI: My companions will come in their own time. I am a solitary sort of person. I like to travel alone. It's faster.
FANG: [*Cleverly*] But then you have no one to talk to!

The listening monks laugh.

BODHI: There is always the Buddha within.

They stop laughing and exchange glances, shamed.

FANG: Do you always move ahead of your companions?
BODHI: Not necessarily ahead but separately. I prefer not to be distracted by idle conversation.
FANG: And what do you like to observe when you are alone?
BODHI: Nature.
FANG: [*Again cleverly*] Are you a poet? Do you mean the scenery?

The two monks snigger.

BODHI: And how the wind blows. And the rose grows. And how different creatures defend and attack.
FANG: So you have an interest in violence?
BODHI: In order to prevent it, deflect it and refuse it.
FANG: What do you mean, refuse it?
BODHI: Everything you receive is a gift so, if you do not accept it, who does it belong to? If someone gives you a kick and you do not take it, where does it go?

Puzzled, Fang Chang and the monks look at each other. Bodhidharma picks up his stick and sandals in preparation to leaving.

FANG: But we are attacked here all the time. By bandits and local ruffians.

BODHI: By being afraid you participate in receiving the attack. Go beyond fear and it will leave you unaffected. Never initiate an attack but learn to return it.

He bows and turns to leave.

FANG: Big talk with little substance. How can we return the attack? We're monks, we're not competent to—

Just then there is a loud commotion and four men, one carrying a wine-jug and another drinking from a cup, enter laughing.

FANG: Dear lord! It's the local ruffians!

Fang Chang and the two monks panic and start scurrying about in fear. Bodhidharma stands where he is bemused, observing the scene. The four ruffians run about laughing and striking at random, scaring Fang and his monks like fluttering pigeons.

RUFFIAN 1: Let's see what the collections were like in the temple....You fat Shaolin baby! We haven't collected for a week!

They laugh and are moving away together, past the cowering Fang and monks, when one of the ruffians notices Bodhidharma.

RUFFIAN 2: Wait! Here's someone new.
RUFFIAN 3: A visitor.
RUFFIAN 1: Which means he is carrying enough to bring him here. Maybe even gold.
RUFFIAN 2: Those sandals must be special if he carries them on a stick.

They laugh.

RUFFIAN 4: Monk, my friend likes your sandals and I like your stick.
RUFFIAN 3: We would like to take them from you.
BODHI: You must either earn or beg. Then, if you receive, it is truly yours.
RUFFIAN 1: A free sermon, along with the gifts we are to get.

They laugh again.

RUFFIAN 4: Lay them down on the ground.

Bodhidharma puts the stick and sandals on the ground.

RUFFIAN 2: Now then, what else do you have?
BODHI: Only my skill.
RUFFIAN 1: [*Laughs*] Show us what skill.
BODHI: I am bound by an oath not to use it unless there is danger.
RUFFIAN 4: There is, indeed, danger.
BODHI: I think not.

They look at each other.

RUFFIAN 3: No danger, you say? Here we are four men and you alone. Do you not feel danger?
BODHI: None.

The cowering monks seem to be urging Fang Chang to speak up. He calls out to Bodhidharma.

FANG: Sir, I suggest you retire. These are not men of peace. They are dangerous.

RUFFIAN 1: Alright, Fang Chang. That's enough out of you!

Fang Chang goes quiet.

RUFFIAN 4: [*To Bodhidharma*] Here is a dagger. [*He draws it*] Is this not dangerous?

BODHI: Yes.

RUFFIAN 4: What if I cut your throat ... like this.

He rushes at Bodhidharma who swiftly disarms him and throws away the dagger.

BODHI: Only weak men need weapons.

They look at each other.

RUFFIAN 1: He insults us!

They rush at him. He strikes variously in all four directions leaving them in different stages of collapse. Then he picks up his stick and sandals and walks away. Fang Chang and the monks, open-mouthed and astounded, inch forward to centrestage and gape at the fallen ruffians. The lights fade.

Scene 4

A large golden image of the Buddha before which a clay lamp burns. Hui K'o with Fang Chang the Abbot of Shaolin Monastery.

HUI: Abbot Fang Chang, it is only right that you should invite Ta-Mo to leave the cave and take up residence here.

FANG: Ever since that day, nine years ago, I've tried, Hui K'o, but — rain or shine, sleet or snow — he won't leave that cave for this place.

HUI: We must find a way to convince him. After all, the other monks from Yindu are here. So am I. It is only proper that he should be here among us.

FANG: But Bo-ti Ta-Mo sits staring at the wall of the cave, reading no scriptures, expounding no commentaries. Our Chinese monks call him the 'pi-kuan Brahmin', the wall-staring Brahmin. Sometimes I wonder, what kind of influence would he have on our monks?

HUI: He is a remarkable man. He speaks little but precisely. He teaches by example. What he does goes beyond books and learning by rote. No one dares disturb him in his cave, except that fellow Vellu.

FANG: Vellu?

HUI: Vellu is the monk who goes around hooded and—

FANG: That's another strange one, like a shadow among shadows. [*Glances offstage*] Ah, there he is — flitting about like a bat avoiding the light.

HUI: He has some affliction, won't expose his body to the sun or the open air. He is most upset that Ta-Mo is not here with us. He climbs to the cave everyday to make some kind of herbal brew that Ta-Mo loves. He carries the ingredients in a pouch at his waist.

FANG: Call him in.

HUI: Your Holiness?

FANG: Bring him to me.

Hui K'o bows and goes out quickly. The Abbot turns to pray to the image of the Buddha.

FANG: O Lord, enable me to penetrate the mystery of this man Bo-ti Ta-Mo and his followers. Help me to understand.

Hui K'o enters with Vellu.

HUI: Your Holiness.
FANG: [*To Vellu*] This is the prayer room. Here you must uncover your head. You are standing before the Lord Buddha.

Vellu hesitates then drops the hood to reveal a shaven head. The Abbot circles Vellu.

FANG: You do not bathe by the well with the other monks. You carry buckets of water and wash yourself where you may not be seen by other eyes. Why?
VELLU: My skin ... cannot stand the light.
FANG: You are ... a very delicately-built man.
VELLU: I come from a delicately-built family.
FANG: Hui K'o says Ta-Mo crossed the Yang-tse on a reed. What do you say?
VELLU: Well, he certainly didn't take the ferry and he didn't swim.
FANG: [*Slightly annoyed*] You are very quick to answer.
VELLU: Part of our training. [*Claps twice and points*]
FANG: [*Puzzled*] What is that?
VELLU: Prajna's method of making you quick-witted.

FANG: Who is Prajna?

VELLU: Bodhidharma's guru, his teacher.

FANG: So ... [*He claps twice and points*]. This makes me quick-witted?

VELLU: No, no. The other person. You have to ask a question, then clap and point like this. [*To Hui*] What was Bodhidharma's answer to you when you asked him to come down from the cave and teach you? [*Claps and points at Hui*]

HUI: Not till the snow turns red.

VELLU: It is snowing now. What will you do? [*Claps and points*]

HUI: Turn the snow red.

VELLU: How? [*Claps and points*]

HUI: [*Thinks quickly, then*] With my blood.

VELLU: [*Claps just once and opens her hands*] There! That is the answer then. Hui K'o has to prove his sincerity. Bodhidharma needs proof of his earnestness. Now, Hui'ko knew that somewhere inside himself but he refused to face it. This intuitive jump brought the realization to the fore. He *realized* it.

Hui K'o and the Abbot look at each other, impressed.

FANG: Very, very interesting. Now tell me, what are the other methods that Ta-Mo uses.

HUI: [*Encouragingly, to Vellu*] His Holiness may ask Ta-Mo to teach all the monks of Shaolin.

VELLU: Like his guru Prajna, he teaches by *kahani* and *katha*.

FANG: *Ko-ani? Kata?*
HUI: What is a *ko-ani?*
VELLU: A very short story that makes you jump from thinking to awareness.
FANG: For instance?
VELLU: A notorious dacoit, who had murdered many people and terrorized a little village in the jungle, heard that the Buddha was coming there to speak. He came to the Buddha and said, 'Be especially respectful of me, I can do anything here.' The Buddha bowed, broke a leaf off a tree and said, "Here, grow this back for me.

A pause. They think about it. The Abbot nods.

FANG: Wonderful! But are all the *ko-ans* about Lord Buddha?
VELLU: No. Whoever has a deep understanding of life may make a wise response that creates a *kahani* worth telling.
FANG: And this other form of teaching he practices. The *kata*. What is that?
VELLU: Stories that you participate in and perform.
FANG: Hm.
HUI: How?
VELLU: He'll show you when you persuade him to teach you.
HUI: I'll go now.
FANG: Carry my greetings and a request. If he agrees to teach you, Hui K'o, say we beg him humbly to teach us all at Shaolin-se. Let him be Abbot in my place.

Hui K'o and Vellu bow in preparation to leaving.

FANG: One last thing, Vellu. When we meditate we sometimes fall asleep but he—?

VELLU: Practices *dhyan*. Focus. Clarity of mind. The emptiness that is full. *Dhyan*.

FANG: *Zya-zan*. This *zya-zen* is done with eyes open?

VELLU: But looking in. So the eyes are half open.

FANG: They say he never shuts his eyes? Some say he has cut off his eyelids?

VELLU: [*Smiles*] These stories grow. But I know he is as human as the rest of us.

FANG: Then how does he stay alert for hours on end?

VELLU: [*Takes something out of a pouch*] Because of this.

HUI: [*Touching them*] Two brown, curled-up things.

FANG: [*Touching them. Withdraws*] The eyelids of Bo-ti Ta-Mo!

VELLU: No, no, no. Two dried and curled, tender leaves of a plant. He drinks a brew called cha.

Hui K'o and the Abbot exchange a glance.

FANG: Cha!

The lights fade.

Scene 5

Outside the cave. It is snowing. Hui K'o is standing in the snow. Bodhidharma can be seen seated cross-legged inside, with his face to the wall of the cave, meditating.

HUI: Master, will you not relent? Please teach me and the monks of Shaolin. Fang Chang wishes you to take over as Abbot of the temple. I have been standing in the snow now for more hours than I can remember. My limbs are freezing. Give me some answer.

BODHI: [*Without turning round*] Do not disturb me or yourself. Go back to the temple.

HUI: Master, it is not easy... but I am determined. Master, you had said, 'Not till the snow turns red.' And I have been building up my courage to do so.

BODHI: No one can do so. Snow is always white. Go on down. Return to the warmth of the temple.

HUI: Master, if you keep your face averted, how can I show you the snow turning red? Look at me, Master. I beseech you. Not since I was a General in the Army have I worn a sword. But I do so today. Master, I beg you. Look. Now!

He draws the sword. At the sound Bodhidharma turns and is on his feet in a split second.

BODHI: No!

The blade flashes as Hui K'o brings the sword down, severing his own left arm at the elbow. Blood spills onto the snow.

BODHI: Oh my God! Here, put ice. Put snow on the wound.

Bodhidharma frantically does so, picking up ice and snow, enclosing the wound.

ACT TWO | 81

HUI: Master, the snow has turned red.

Bodhidharma embraces him.

BODHI: Hui K'o! Hui K'o! Hui K'o!

The lights fade.

Scene 6

A shaken Bodhidharma stands beside Abbot Fang Chang who is seated on the stump of a tree in the courtyard of the Shaolin Temple addressing the monks, some of whom can be seen onstage.

BODHI: I start my teaching here in the temple by doing honour first to Hui K'o. He proved his sincerity by a method so extreme that I am deeply moved and shaken. He turned the snow red with his own blood by cutting off his left arm.

Nods and murmurs of awe among the monks.

BODHI: It saddens me. It is not an example to emulate. I am sure he will soon recover from the loss of blood. But he will never recover his lost limb. To honour the strength of Hui K'o's determination, let us all vow that, as of today, we, the monks of Shaolin, will greet each other and the world only with the right hand — thus!

He does a one-handed namaskar and the monks do the same.

BODHI: Abbot Fang Chang has done me great honour by handing to my charge the care of the monastery of Shaolin. Therefore, I ask him where I should begin.

FANG: [*Stands up*] O Ta-Mo, begin by satisfying our curiosity. Many of us have seen you practise on the open ground outside the cave what seemed like a graceful dance. When I asked some monks from Yindu about it, they said you had converted an oral tradition of Yindu into one without words. They called it your *kata* of action. We would be honoured if you could show us today your Zen Katha.

The seated monks nod and applaud to indicate their approval. Abbot Fang Chang resumes his seat on the tree stump. Bodhidharma now performs what appears to be a highly stylized, ritualistic, choreographed set of movements displaying agility and vigour punctuated by explosive releases of breath. When he concludes, he bows. The monks in the audience applaud.

BODHI: You applaud what you see because it seems beautiful and graceful, a sort of dance of Nataraja. But it is more than that. It is the *katha* of how I was attacked and how I defended myself.

Two or three monks raise their hands to ask questions. Bodhidharma points to one of them.

MONK 1: We have heard that *zen* is taught by *ko-an* and *kata*. What is the difference between a *ko-an* and a *kata*?

BODHI: A *kahani* is a story that makes you think; a *katha* is a story in which you must perform. Both guide you towards *dhyan*.

MONK 2: Master, you just showed us a *kata*. Where was the story in that?

BODHI: Ah. That is where knowledge and imagination supply the link. But no words are spoken.

MONK 1: Please explain, Master.

BODHI: Very well. What I performed was the story of what happened right here in this courtyard when I first arrived. Do you remember what happened?

MONK 1: Four ruffians attacked you.

BODHI: Correct. But I showed you only my side of the action. So it was only one side of the *katha*. For it to be whole, you must participate in the imagination. To help you this time, I will ask four of you to participate in the performance. [*He selects four of the monks*] You. You. You. And you. [*He picks up a small, short wooden baton about eight inches long and hands it to one of the participants.*] Assume this is the dagger in the hand of the first attacker, and the others will attack from other directions. When you are ready, begin!

They attack just as the ruffians had done in the earlier scene. Bodhidharma repeats the actions of the katha, vanquishing his attackers. Bodhidharma helps them up while Vellu also helps revive and reassure them. They now sit onstage. Bodhidharma resumes addressing the audience.

BODHI: In my cave, I wondered why *katha* should not be used to help train you in the martial art techniques I have devised. After all, in India we use the *katha* form for imparting knowledge of the scriptures and epics. So I have adapted *katha* to this purpose.

MONK 1: [*Raising a hand*] Does one require *zyan* for the martial arts?

BODHI: Oh definitely. *Dhyan* focuses the mind. Keeps you calm. You hear the universal music. You flow gracefully like water.

MONK 2: Like water? But, Ta-Mo, should we not learn to be as firm as rock?

BODHI: No. Have the strength of water. Rock breaks. Water can destroy. Flow round and upon everything.

MONK 3: Your *zen kata*, will we all learn it?

BODHI: [*Smiles*] Of course. But it begins with proper breathing. As a child, I was weak and out of breath. I almost died. It was my guru, Prajnaratna, who studied the problem and realized that a new-born baby cries, not to breathe in but to breathe out — to expel the stale air trapped in its lungs. So, first, we must learn to breathe out correctly in order to coordinate the energy of mind and body, and focus it with *dhyan*, so that we move with greater understanding of the cosmic *katha*.

The lights fade.

Scene 7

The Emperor and Courtier 1.

EMPEROR: You are sure the news is accurate? Ta-Mo is working miracles in Shaolin?

COURTIER 1: Sire. Within a short period of Bodhidharma taking charge of the monastery of Shaolin, not only have the monks routed the bandits who attacked, they have swept down the mountain and cleared the village of the ruffians and brigands who bothered the peasant folk. The villagers now visit the temple of Shaolin on every holiday. Hundreds gather to hear the teachings of the Buddha.

EMPEROR: Which scriptures does Ta-Mo teach?

COURTIER 1: Many. But he says enlightenment doesn't come out of scripture or ritual recitation but out of *dhyan*.

EMPEROR: So with this zen, at any time, any person can be enlightened?

COURTIER 1: Suddenly. Unexpectedly. In the middle of routine work. Bodhidharma emphasizes the importance of one's ordinary daily work. Without ego. Without attachment to reward. Even if it is just sweeping the house.

EMPEROR: Ah. Perhaps his zen has now reached our understanding.

COURTIER 1: Sire?

EMPEROR: An Emperor too must work without ego and expectation of reward, whether in this life or the next. [*A pause*] Send a messenger to Shaolin. Say Emperor Wu-ti's eyes have been opened. He begs Ta-Mo's pardon.

The lights fade.

Scene 8

The warrior monks of Shaolin stand in disciplined ranks. Bodhidharma stands before them.

BODHI: Remember, take as thought the thought of no-thought. Empty the mind, mind the empty. See rest in motion and motion in rest. [*Turns to them*] Begin.

The Katha begins. The troupe executes the movements in graceful coordination and unison.

They execute it. When it is done, Bodhidharma rises and speaks to them.

BODHI: Any questions?
MAN 2: Master, what is the best preparation for combat?
BODHI: Calm the fluttering mind
    that wants to take off
    like a bird scared.

    Relax and let it flow, let go
    intuition's arrow from the bow
    for the mind is focused, on target.

    Follow through, completely aware
    that what you do later also affects
    the flight of that which went before.

MAN 3: So what we do before affects what happens after, even when we are physically not there?

BODHI: [*Smiles*] Like *karma*. For instance, when you strike, if the fist is turning, the blow reaches in deep and the energy continues turning within.

MAN 2: What you say is sometimes so deep we cannot fully understand it.

BODHI: After learning, go outside words, within to wisdom.

MAN 2: Master, sometimes I am distracted by thought.

BODHI: Set it down.

MAN 2: How?

BODHI: Two monks were about to cross a stream. They saw a beautiful woman. The younger monk would not help her across. The elder picked her up in his arms and carried her over and set her down. That night the young monk complained before the gathering of monks that the elder had held a woman close that day. The elder replied: I set her down on the other bank but you are still carrying her.

Laughter. The lights fade.

Scene 9

Night. By the light of a few oil lamps, Vellu is looking at himself in a hand-mirror. In a moment, his unhappiness with his appearance becomes evident. He looks left and right quickly to ensure he is alone, then proceeds to undo a little bundle from which he withdraws whatever he requires to transform himself again into a semblance of the Sanghameeta now buried in the monk. He drapes a piece of silk over himself, and studies and enjoys the effect. Then he adorns himself with a ring and other trinkets. Finally, he takes from the bundle the glittering Diamond Fist and hangs it from a chain about his neck. It makes a magnificent ornament.

There is a stealthy knocking sound. Vellu is now in consternation. He extinguishes all but one of the lamps, then rushes about and takes cover.

A monk enters and searches quietly among the shadows for Vellu who, in turn, keeps moving out of sight. Eventually, the monk who has entered picks up the lamp as though to use it for better visibility. This reveals his face. Seeing that it is Vajra, Vellu steps out of the shadows.

VELLU: Vajra! For heaven's sake, identify yourself before you come creeping in like that.

VAJRA: Vellu... I mean, Sangha, why are you dressed up like that?

VELLU: I was just …. remembering.

VELLU: [*Begins taking off the trinkets and adornments*] Why are you here? You're not supposed to leave your cell and go snooping about at night.

VAJRA: To see you and warn you. You remember how old Fang Chang the previous Abbot grilled you once? Well, Hui K'o told me today that Fang Chang actually asked Bodhidharma about you.

VELLU: What did he ask?

VAJRA: This is most awkward for me.

VELLU: No, no, tell me. I was with them all day in the forest picking herbs and mushrooms. No one said anything to me.

VAJRA: Apparently, Fang Chang noticed that while all the monks just stood and made water wherever they wanted to, you went and squatted behind a bush.

VELLU: How stupid of me! That's a silly mistake. What did Bodhidharma say?

VAJRA: He said men in India sometimes squatted, sometimes stood. But he agreed that, generally, men did it as if they were plucking flowers and women as if they were picking herbs. There were other things they had noticed too... the pitch of your voice, the effeminacy of your gestures. The fact that you never bared your chest even at martial arts practice.

VELLU: Do you think I'm on the verge of getting caught? Vajra what shall I do?

VAJRA: Run away with me. My sister and brother-in-law are right here in China. They'll look after us. We have property here. We could get married, settle down. Even go back to Kanchi, if that's what you want.

VELLU: I came here for Bodhidharma. I did this for him.

VAJRA: You are like a moth around a flame. You will only burn yourself to death.

VELLU: I must not fail him.

VAJRA: But, you must be true to yourself. Look at what you were doing a little while ago, harking back to the reality of your being. Why should you hide yourself as a man when you are a woman?

VELLU: For him.

VAJRA: Ha, he doesn't want it! You've tied yourself up in your own lie. Go to him, tell him the truth. I suspect he already knows it.

VELLU: Dare I?

VAJRA: Of course. We all learn and grow and find ourselves anew. Look at me. How angry I used to be! Now, here, in the quiet of the monastery I've begun to understand myself. Looking deep into my being as into a well, I have seen a distant face reflected but I wasn't sure it was me. I realized, if I disturbed the water, I couldn't see myself, but if I was still, so was the water and I could. Here, through dhyan, I have learnt to be still.

VELLU: [*Smiles*] You're becoming quite poetic. But I always knew your anger was a cry for help for someone to love you.

VAJRA: I hated myself.

VELLU: There, you see. Even you didn't like yourself. You were like a spoilt child throwing tantrums, hoping someone would rescue you.

VAJRA: [*Half-joking*] Then why didn't you extend a hand to me?

VELLU: [*Turns away*] I think you should go now.

VAJRA: My brother-in-law is coming to see me tomorrow. Would you like to send a message for your father?

VELLU: You know my answer.

VAJRA: That answer is not yours, it is Bodhidharma's. Because he says, 'Externally, keep yourself away from all relationships, internally have no longings' you are trying to suppress your real feelings.

VELLU: That's not true.

Vajra enfolds Vellu in his arms from behind.

VAJRA: Sangha don't deny yourself.

Vellu breaks free.

VELLU: You trouble me.

VAJRA: Sublimating your sexuality won't solve anything. We have to learn to know ourselves.

He looks at her for a moment. Then goes. The lights fade.

Scene 10

Morning. Bodhidharma at work on a manuscript. Vellu enters.

VELLU: Master, I have a confession to make. [*Bodhidharma looks at Vellu*] I fear discovery. The consequences will be terrible.

BODHI: I see.

VELLU: I am a woman.

BODHI: Hm.

VELLU: Aren't you upset? Aren't you going to get angry with me?

BODHI: For what? For being a woman?

VELLU: [*Dumbfounded*] I don't understand.
BODHI: I do.
VELLU: Did you suspect? Did you know?
BODHI: Does it matter?
VELLU: No. No. I suppose not. I... I shall continue as I am. You realize, I am your own Sanghameeta?
BODHI: I see.
VELLU: Does it not matter to you?
BODHI: If it does, it does. If it doesn't, it doesn't.
VELLU: When shall I reveal myself? When shall I tell everyone?
BODHI: When it suits you. We all have our decisions to make and must not surrender that strength. [*Smiles*] I too have just made a decision. Find Vajra and take him along to the main prayer hall. Hui K'o is waiting there for me. I shall be there shortly.

The lights fade.

Scene 11

Before the large golden statue of the seated Buddha, Hui K'o is praying with his jade beads in his right hand. The lower half of his left sleeve hangs empty.

HUI: *Om mane padme hom. Om mane padme hom. Buddham sharanam gachami! Dhamam sharanam gachami! Sangham sharanam gachami!*

Vajra and Vellu enter and bow with joined hands to the Buddha. Hui K'o gets up anxiously and turns to them.

HUI: Vellu! Vajra! We must do something about it.
VAJRA: About what?
HUI: I was with him in the dining hall when a young monk who had joined today, asked him to teach him zen. Bodhidharma looked at me and nodded. I asked the young man, "Have you finished eating?" He said, yes. I said, "Here is your first lesson in zen: wash your bowl."
VELLU: Excellent!
VAJRA: What did Bodhidharma say to that?
HUI: He said he was now sure that the teaching was in safe hands.
VELLU: He told me he had come to some decision.
HUI: [*To Vajra*] I know you've always thought of me as an idiot and now you probably think I'm a one-armed idiot but I've always felt we had much in common.
VAJRA: [*To Vellu*] It just shows how I've progressed. I can't tell whether I'm being insulted or not. And it doesn't matter anymore.
HUI: Ta-Mo is from your country. You will perhaps know better than me what he means. I need to know how I should react.
VELLU: Hui K'o, please explain yourself.
HUI: It's most distressing! Most upsetting! We must do something about it. Ta-Mo says his work here is done.
VAJRA: That's exactly what I feel. He's taught everyone *dhyan*. He's delivered sermons. He's made Shaolin monks — even those who were fat and slobbery — into the most deadly fighters in the world. He's handed on his

classic exercises for breathing power, muscle change, and the Eighteen Hand Movements that repel all attack. What more do you want?

HUI: We want him to stay. He's coming here now to inform you of his decision. Please. Please. Tell him we need him.

VELLU: Why don't you tell him yourself?

HUI: I did. And he said, "Consider me dead and continue. I have done what I came here to do. Death overtakes mortals in mid-stride. I would like to welcome it." It almost broke my heart. I couldn't hold back the tears. To think of our Master as dead! Stop him from taking this step. Vajra, Vellu, you must persuade him not to do it.

VAJRA: [*Worriedly*] Indian yogis sometimes go into *samadhi*, burying themselves alive.

VELLU: But those are the ones who can stop their pulse and breathing for days on end. And then they emerge, out of the earth, refreshed and rested as though after a sleep.

Bodhidharma enters. He carries a stick over his shoulder with two sandals dangling from it. Behind him comes Fang Chang who had been the Abbot before him.

HUI: Master, Master, my mind is most agitated. Calm it for me.

BODHI: I will. [*Holds out his hands to receive*] If you first bring me your mind.

Hui K'o looks about at a loss for an answer.

ACT TWO | 95

HUI: Master, I cannot find it.
BODHI: Then there is nothing to calm. Now it is time for me to go.
VAJRA: This is most sudden.
BODHI: Life is sudden. So is death.
VELLU: I have a question. Is it because they are beginning to treat you like a god?
BODHI: Perhaps. [*To Hui*] Go, gather the monks of Shaolin. I give you this sandal so that you may conduct my funeral ceremonies over it.

He hands him one of the sandals.

HUI: [*Falling to his knees*] Master!

He takes the sandal and placing it on the ground, touches his head to the floor before it. Then Hui takes the sandal and touches it to his forehead.

VAJRA: Your funeral ceremonies?
HUI: Master, what shall I say to the monks?
BODHI: Accept death in life. Realize that chasing nirvana is a desire. Both must come, sometimes together, sometimes one before the other. There is no duality. All is one.
VAJRA: Master, Vellu and I were wondering if—
BODHI: [*Holds up his hand*] It happened that a monk fell in love with a nun and sent her a written declaration of devotion. Later that day when all the monks had gathered for prayers, she stood up and said, "One person here has written me a love letter. Let him stand up now if he dares and embrace me."

VELLU: Did he?
VAJRA: Did she?
FANG: Did the other monks permit it?
BODHI: Ask Hui K'o. It happened in his monastery across the river.

They look at him. Hui K'o smiles. Bodhidharma smiles and turns to leave.

FANG: After you are gone, who will be Abbot in your place?
BODHI: Ah, yes. Let me ask all of you. While I was here, what have you learned about the Way? [*Turns to Vajra*] Tell me.
VAJRA: Words alone are not enough.
BODHI: You have brushed my skin.

He looks at Vellu.

VELLU: A vision of the Truth can be a glimpse of eternal paradise.
BODHI: You have touched my flesh.
FANG: All is nothingness.
BODHI: You have reached my bone.

Bodhidharma looks at Hui K'o who merely comes up to him and bows with eyes on him, straightens up and goes back to his place.

BODHI: [*To Hui K'o*] You *are* my marrow. I appoint you Abbot in my place. I came here as 28th Patriarch of Buddhism and leave as the 1st Patriarch of Dhyan. Or

Chan, as you call it here. I now give you, Hui K'o, my mantle and confer on you the title 2nd Patriarch of Chan.

The lights fade.

Scene 12

The Emperor and Courtier 1.

EMPEROR: Dead? Bo-ti Ta-Mo dead! How can that be? Did some bandit kill him?
COURTIER 1: No, no, Sire. It seems he died of his own volition. He willed it.
EMPEROR: Hm. Most strange.
COURTIER 1: Our messenger actually saw the smoke rising from the funeral pyre. So the peasant folk have begun saying Bodhidharma rose to heaven in a column of smoke. Because they saw no body, no corpse, on the pyre. But... but, Sire, what is most amazing is that ....
EMPEROR: Why do you tremble and stop?
COURTIER 1: Sire... Sire... Our messenger was so intrigued by these events that he ... he broke into the memorial the monks have built to house the ashes of Bodhidharma—
EMPEROR: What? Desecrated a tomb? Broke into a sacred resting-place! This is a sacrilege against the ashes of Ta-Mo!
COURTIER 1: But, Sire, there were no ashes there.
EMPEROR: No ashes? No bones? No teeth? No skull?

COURTIER 1: No, Sire. Only a single foot-worn sandal.
EMPEROR: A single sandal. What does it mean?
COURTIER 1: Our messenger says he is sure that, while the entire countryside was grieving for the passing away of Bodhidharma, he saw the very image of him walking towards the snow mountains, with a stick over his shoulder and one sandal hanging from it.
EMPEROR: Ah.
COURTIER 1: At first he thought he was seeing a ghost. And then he saw the two other monks from Yindu following him.
EMPEROR: Well, well, well! Has there been any other sighting of this ... this phenomenon?
COURTIER 1: Sire. Our Ambassador to Yindu who has returned this evening, says he saw a man carrying a stick and sandal, leading a small group of monks, through a high pass, towards the treacherous sands of the Telemaken Desert. He said to me that he thought it was Bodhidharma. In fact, he spoke to him, Sire.
EMPEROR: Was it or was it not Ta-Mo? Tell the Ambassador to seek an audience with us tomorrow. We must know for certain. Why is he so unsure?
COURTIER 1: Because, Sire, he has heard that Bodhidharma is dead and cremated. The Ambassador is a senior Civil Servant. He doesn't want people to say he is seeing ghosts or hallucinating. [*Bows*]

The lights fade.

Scene 13

A misty plateau in the high mountains. Bodhidharma, carrying a stick with one sandal dangling from it, enters followed by Vajra and Vellu walking slowly as though after much climbing.

BODHI: [*Breathes deep*] Ah, how fresh and invigorating the air is! That is how you will feel when you are yourself again.

VELLU: I will be more myself than ever before. I have gained a glimpse of eternity.

VAJRA: And I am at peace with myself.

BODHI: That's good news for the world.

They all laugh.

VELLU: As you suggested, I shall choose my moment to delight and surprise my father. I shall reveal myself as Sanghameeta when I am before him.

BODHI: He will be pleased that Vajra brings you home. [*Smiles*] Or, rather, that you bring *him* home. [*Looks ahead of him*] Well, here our paths diverge. You both go down this way, through the passes and on to Kanchi. I move on that way to unknown places.

VELLU: Must you go?

BODHI: [*Nods*] The Buddha said, "Each one must work out his own salvation and be a lamp unto himself." [*Starts leaving*] This is my path. You and Vajra have chosen wisely too.

VELLU: [*Begins crying*] We won't be able to stop thinking of you.

BODHI: [*Stops*] Think of me only as another who came and went this way.

She moves forward to touch his feet. Vajra follows suit. But Bodhidharma moves back.

BODHI: No, no, no. [*Carefully, clearly, slowly*] Atma, mahatma, anatma. In the one, no one.

He does the one-handed Shaolin namaskar open-eyed and walks away into the mist. Vellu is crying but trying hard not to. Vajra holds Vellu to him.

CURTAIN